CANDACE CAMERON BURE

with Darlene Schacht

Reshaping It ALL

Motivation for Physical and Spiritual Fitness

PUBLISHING GR
Nashville, Ten

978-1-4336-6973-6

Published by B&H Publishing Group
Nashville, Tennessee

Dewey Decimal Classification: 613.2
Subject Heading: FOOD ADDICTION \ PHYSICAL
FITNESS \ SPIRITUAL LIFE

Unless otherwise noted, Scripture quotations are from the
Holy Bible, New International Version, copyright © 1973, 1978,
1984 by International Bible Society.

Also used: New King James Version (NKJV), copyright © 1979,
1980, 1982, Thomas Nelson, Inc., Publishers.

Also used: New American Standard Bible (NASB),
© the Lockman Foundation, 1960, 1962, 1963, 1968, 1971, 1972,
1973, 1975, 1977; used by permission.

Also used: *The Message*, the New Testament in Contemporary
English, © 1993 by Eugene H. Peterson, published by NavPress,
Colorado Springs, Colorado.

Also used: The King James Version (KJV). Public domain.

1 2 3 4 5 6 7 8 • 14 13 12 11

This book is dedicated to the countless women and gentlemen who have written me through the years struggling not only with their weight, but with their spiritual life. You're the reason my thoughts, stories, defeats, and triumphs have been penned. I pray that in sharing some of my experiences it will encourage and inspire you in bigger ways than you could have imagined.

Acknowledgments

From Candace:

To the Lord of my life, Jesus Christ—is thank You enough? You have rocked my world, literally, and flipped it upside down. I'm forever grateful for Your opening my eyes. You're taking me on a journey I'd never have imagined for myself. No matter where life leads or what You allow for me, You are ALWAYS good.

Val—the love of my life. You've not only helped me keep an active, healthy, and fit lifestyle, but you've helped me enjoy it along the way. Thank you for waking me up gently on mornings I've wanted to sleep in, thank you for running at a slower pace just so we could spend time working out together, and thank you for being a leading example to me and our children.

Natasha, Lev, and Maksim—my little ducklings. I hope that one day when you're older, this book will help remind you of all the principles your Papa and I have tried to teach you over the years. It's not always fun to be disciplined about exercise and the foods we put into our body, but it's well worth it in the end. Remember that your body is a holy temple for God to move through. Keep it strong and keep it healthy for Jesus! Thank you for giving me fun stories to share with others. You've taught me more than you'll ever know. I love you with all my heart.

Ford and Jeffery—the best managers and friends one could ask for. You've always represented me with integrity, heart, class, and concern for the bigger picture. Thank you for always understanding my boundaries, limitations, and heart's desires in this crazy entertainment industry. Thank you for your relentless pursuit to seek and create projects for me that will make a difference and for always having my back. Especially when having my back means delivering this pregnant girl food in the middle of an N'Sync concert!

Jennifer Lyell—you've been more than a delight to me and I can't thank you enough for making my first publishing experience super enjoyable. Thank you for praying for me and seeking me out and thanks to everyone at B&H Publishing Group for believing in me and my ministry. I'm looking forward to seeing what the future holds.

Mom and Dad—you truly are my heroes. Mom, you have the biggest heart of any woman I know, and you are the world's best cheerleader. I'm happy I've inherited that part of you as I cheer on my own family. Dad, we get each other. I love your sense of humor and the way you make me laugh. I couldn't have asked God for any better parents than He gave me. I love you both.

Melissa—it's the same, but different. . . . Seriously, I don't know that I've personally seen anyone transform their life the way you have. You've encouraged me to be a better mother and to go deeper with the Lord because of seeing the godly woman you've become.

Bridgette—oh yes, baby, oh yes! Bridgie, I love spending time with you and am so proud of the leader you've become in your Mom to Mom group. Remember, you're Barbara Mandrell, Melissa is Louise, and I'm Irlene.

Kirk—thank you for sharing with me *The Way of the Master* by Ray Comfort. It opened my eyes to the true gospel and I'm forever grateful. Your family and ministry have set the bar high and continue to inspire me in my walk with Christ.

Dilini—my BFF since the tenth grade. I'm so glad we're beyond walking from store to store getting the most fattening foods as possible and pigging out! Although it was fun when we were eighteen. Here's to keeping each other on track, motivating one another to eat clean, and exercise at least three times a week, and not calling ourselves bad names when we're having puffy day—we are ONLY God's glorious and beautiful girls!

Pete Steinfeld—you gave me the foundation on which to build a healthy body. Thank you for all the expertise, unexpected check up phone calls, motivation, and drive to get my butt moving in the early days.

Stacy Carto—your words have impacted my life more than you'll ever know. Thank you for being obedient to God as well as open and honest to a girl you barely knew. You can expect a huge jewel in your crown for that one!

Darlene Schacht—without whom this book wouldn't be possible. It feels like yesterday you were interviewing me for CWO and now we've published a book together! We're like Thelma and Louise, two women on life's journey together except we've found the secret to it all: Jesus Christ. You're writing has wowed me and I couldn't be more proud of you. Your biblical knowledge and discernment has caused me to listen harder and reach farther than I've ever dreamed. Thank you from the bottom of my heart. I think we make a pretty good team.

My shout-outs of gratitude to all those who have contributed to this book in one way or another—Redrock Entertainment Development; James at Anderson Group PR; Naomi and Emily at Ambassador Speakers Bureau; Tara Brooks: thanks for always making me look my best; Mikel Healey: you're a brilliant photographer; and Laura Corby: love your style. Susan Loggans and Dennis Watson: thank you for allowing me to use your beautiful home for the cover photo. To all my Bible study girlfriends who've prayed me through the thought of this book to it's completion: Debbie, Kim, Linda, Ann, Beth, Terri, and Julie. Also, my prayer warrior Stacy W. Much love to pastor Bob and Calvary Chapel in Ft. Lauderdale. Speed, Lisa, Alex, and Mandy: you know I love ya! Tom Caton, for your heart and always making me smile on set, Oh my soul! And my special friend Angela Glover: who warmly reminds me that no matter how important exercise is, it's never more important than my time alone with God. You are a gift from God to me.

From Darlene:

I'd like to thank my niece, writing partner, and friend, Stephanie Fries, for reviewing my rough drafts and for her constant readiness to help. Her attention to detail has been my greatest asset as a writer. Thank you also to Bonnie Hooley, Phyllis Fieber, and Jane Drul who believed I could write before I believed it was true. I'm grateful for your encouragement and support.

I'd also like to thank Ford Englerth for handling the details of our proposal, and the team at B&H Publishing Group for the tireless work you have done. Like a diamond in the rough, you have carefully handled our book, polishing the words, before presenting it as a sparkling gem.

I owe my sincerest gratitude to Candace Cameron Bure for giving me the opportunity of a lifetime of being her writing partner and friend. I'm blessed beyond words by this woman who spent countless hours in prayer for this book. I'm thankful for my husband Michael whose anchor of faith has kept me grounded and hungry for the Word of God. And to Almighty God who like ink flows through my pen and into each word I write.

Contents

Acknowledgments   v

One: A Full House of My Own   1

Two: The Inside Scoop   11

Three: Grab Wings and Soar   25

Four: Dad's Infinity and Beyond   37

Five: Heads Up, Eyes Forward, Shoulders Back   51

Six: Dressed in Designer Genes   63

Seven: Unlock Your Freedom   77

Eight: Live an Adorable Life   93

Nine: Don't Feed the Lions   107

Ten: Hey There, Delilah   119

Eleven: Reviewing My Script   131

Twelve: Life Is a Glass Jar   143

Thirteen: Discover Contentment   155

Fourteen: Learn the Art of Dining Out   167

Fifteen: A House Swept Clean 179

Sixteen: It Is Well with My Soul 189

Seventeen: Is Meekness a Weakness? 201

Eighteen: Leaving a Legacy 213

Nineteen: Being Good Isn't Good Enough 225

Notes 239

ONE

A Full House of My Own

Two nights ago Mom was in the kitchen when she heard Lev screaming, "Grandma, Grandma!" at the top of his lungs. Actually I think the entire neighborhood heard him. Startled, she ran outside to find Lev, standing on the front porch with tears streaming down his face. Meanwhile, Samson, our friendly canine giant, was proudly standing by, displaying his latest hunting trophy—a Muscovy duck. Make that a dead duck.

It was a little too gruesome for Mom's liking and Lev's sensitive soul too for that matter, who had just witnessed the aftermath of the hunt. Samson's tail didn't skip a beat as it waved a flag, announcing his victory.

Arriving at home, I was addressed by three children and one concerned Grandma who relayed each detail in color. Upon further investigation, we discovered that Samson had tangled with the wrong duck, leaving five orphaned ducklings waiting in a nearby drain for Momma Muscovy to come waddling home.

Now three kids and five ducks were crying, which put a whole new spin on the once cheerful tune, "Six Little Ducks Went Out to Play."

The next morning my daughter Natasha and the neighbors rescued the ducklings, packed their feathered bags, and moved them into our guest room. After all, Val and I only have three kids, three dogs, one hamster, a tortoise, and two busy careers on our plate; what's five more beaks to feed?

After looking into the persuasive eyes of my youngest son, Maks, I agreed to take them in for a week or so but also thought it best to give the Wildlife Center a call. They said to bring the ducklings into the center where they would care for them until it was time to introduce them back into the wild. I got the feeling that their idea of "the wild" was as far away from the Bure family as possible.

We packed the ducks into a cardboard box, along with some grass, a bowl of water, and one of Samson's favorite chew toys (no, not their mother) and made our way out to the car.

Natasha, being the drama queen that she is, cried the entire way there, but once she saw the ducks settling in, she agreed that it was the best plan.

I'm glad we rescued the ducklings, disappointed that my doggie annihilated their mom, and thrilled that I'm not adding five ducks to our already full house. We all miss our feathered little friends, but as cute as they were, that chirping had started to ring in our ears! So there you have a glimpse into the life of a Hollywood star; glamorous, huh?

Life *can* be glamorous at times when I'm traveling to far-off places, shooting a movie, or meeting fellow celebrities, but behind the scenes I live what most would consider an ordinary life:

- I drive my kids to and from school most days.
- I participate in classroom "mom stuff."
- I'm on the board of our school's annual auction committee each year.
- I take our dogs for walks and feed them.
- We eat dinner at home almost every night.
- I work out with friends—not a personal trainer.
- I take an exercise class on Monday mornings in our school gym with a bunch of other moms.
- I'm in charge of paying the bills, writing checks, and filing each month.
- I fly economy most of the time—not first class.
- I shop for our groceries.
- I don't have a nanny, a chef, a personal trainer, a driver, or even a personal assistant (and boy, do I wish I did some days)!
- I mop my floors often because our dogs like to swim in the pool then come in the house wet with mud on their feet—and let's not forget the feathers!
- I'm a stain-removal fanatic, and I'm good at it!
- And like everyone else—I hang out at Starbucks!

Yes, in many ways my life is ordinary, but it's also EXTRAordinary because of my relationship with the Most High God.

I pray this book will be more than a weight-loss book and far more than my testimony. I pray that by it faith will be your compass in this journey through weight loss to freedom, as it has also been mine. Not only is God wanting to walk this journey with you; He is ready to equip you to handle the job. *Why?* Because He is "able to do exceeding abundantly above all that we ask or think, according to the power that works in us" (Eph. 3:20 NKJV). And besides that, He cares so deeply for you that even the hairs on your head are numbered.

I've known God since the age of twelve, but even though I called myself a "Christian" and said the "sinner's prayer," I wasn't living like one. It's different now. Today, rather than just walking alone under the umbrella of grace, I desire to walk there in fellowship with Him—a fellowship that has led me on a journey to freedom in Christ.

I've made many decisions about work because of my Christian walk. I've turned down several TV series to stay at home and raise my children. I've also turned down other roles because of content issues I feel strongly about.

I never thought I'd be someone who'd have the opportunity to speak at churches and share *my* testimony with thousands of people, but I can see now how God is using the success of *Full House* to reach millions of people for Him. How cool is that?

It's not every day that an opportunity like *Full House* comes along, but it did, and I'm glad that I was there to be a part of it all. I loved every day that I spent growing up in front of the camera and working on the set with the others. Acting always has and always will be a passion of mine. However, once family came along, I felt a desire to adjust my priorities.

Marrying an NHL hockey star and having three kids will change anyone's life, and it changed mine immensely. Suddenly I went from being a television star living in Hollywood to starring in my own role as a wife and mother at home with my kids. Because I love my career, the decision to be a stay-at-home mom was a tough one. We were living in Calgary, my oldest child Natasha was born, and I had started meeting with agents in LA again. After being in LA for a week and a half, I realized I was miserable. I hadn't seen my husband Val in ten days, and by the time I'd get home each night, Natasha was already asleep. Anyone who's a mom knows how tough that can be!

Shortly after returning home, Val and I sat down for a talk, and I poured out my thoughts.

Val's response was more than sympathetic, supportive, and encouraging, which was exactly what I needed to hear. While he had been fully supportive of my dreams, part of him quietly hoped I'd come to this conclusion. This reassurance that we were on the same page was great. We both looked forward to the opportunity it offered me to attend his games and keep cheering him on.

Both Val and I have never had a single regret in making our decision. I love working, but I also love the fact that God nudges us along through the seasons of our lives into unexpected places.

That season of my life was wonderful in so many ways; I was a young woman ready to open a new chapter in my life as a wife and a mom. The smile on my face went a long way, but at times it was covering a lot of insecurities and unknowns in my life. It was a season of blessings and a season of struggle, and during that time I took my first steps into the cycle of bulimia.

It started in Montreal. I was nineteen, engaged, and living with Val—as a good Christian girl ought *not* to do. Perhaps if I had been living and walking in faith, I wouldn't have started the cycle of binging and purging. But I did. One would expect that my situation had everything to do with the pin-thin expectations of Hollywood—the desire that so many starlets have to be thin. After all, I did fit the role of DJ Tanner, the sister with the Charlie Brown cheeks, who once went on a crash diet herself. But no, that wasn't me.

It had nothing to do with body image or trying to lose weight but had everything to do with adjustment and fear. As I prepared for marriage, had stopped working (as I had been since I was five), and was living in a foreign city, I felt that I had nothing left of my old life to turn to for balance. I was thrown (albeit, happily) into a world I knew nothing about—a housewife, a hockey wife, and soon after, a mom.

Loneliness set in during those years when Val was on the road, as it does for most hockey wives. We enjoyed wonderful summers together, but his time with the NHL essentially felt like a six-month road trip, at which time I was alone. Had it not been for our telephone calls two to three times a day, I don't know what I would have done.

What I did do is binge. There's something oddly comforting about food or, better said, *the thought of food* that tricks our minds into believing that it can and will fill our void. And so I listened to the lie hoping that it too would fill mine. In the beginning I only did it when Val was on the road—when I was by myself: me, the TV, and my food. One bite, one mouthful, one spoonful, then two . . . until I was disgusted with the amount I'd consumed. Hoping to undo my discomfort and guilt, I would purge.

With all things bad, the more you do it, the more you get wrapped up in it. Thus it started happening when I wasn't alone—until I finally got caught.

There it was, out in the open. I stood face-to-face with my dad, watching him tear up as he discovered my shame. I knew he was afraid and worried for me. And since I love him so much, it broke my heart. I never wanted my actions to hurt the people I love.

English writer, Monica Baldwin writes, "What makes humility so desirable is the marvelous thing it does to us; it creates in us a capacity for the closest possible intimacy with God."

Humiliation depicts mankind as broken and weak before God, yet it holds power and freedom to those it affects. Getting caught, embarrassed, and ashamed was finally the turning point for me. The shame of admitting the lie in my heart was the truth that set me free.

What I didn't realize at the time is that my heart was longing for the things of this world. I ran to comfort food instead of running to God. I discovered my sin, but I hadn't discovered that my heart was in the wrong place. I sought moral reformation instead of a spiritual transformation. I had known who He was, but I still hadn't grasped who I was in His sight.

After reading a book my brother Kirk gave to me, *The Way of the Master* by Ray Comfort, my life and walk with God changed forever! It spoke of the Ten Commandments and revealed my sin in its true light. That day in church—way back when I was twelve—I had prayed the "sinner's prayer," asking God to forgive my sins, but I didn't even understand what my sin was. After holding my life up against the standard of the Ten Commandments, the law revealed my sin, and I went through every commandment, realizing that I had broken them all.

I also realized that God was going to judge me by *this* standard—not by the world's. If we break even the least of His commandments, we have broken His law (James 2:10). It would have been easy had I been able to go on measuring myself against the lives of other Hollywood child stars, but if I had, I wouldn't be walking in the peace and freedom that I am today. Seeing who I am in sin and who I have become through Him has caused me to drop to my knees and ask for forgiveness. I have come to the realization of how amazing God is by sending His Son, Jesus, to pay for *my* sin. That's why I choose to live a life pleasing to God and bask in the grace He gives to each and every one of us.

God has changed me in ways that words cannot describe. He has transformed the way I think and live my life. Things that were once important to me no longer are. I can't help but share that good news with you, how it has set me free, and how it can also free you!

My desire stays strong each and every day because of the gratitude I have in my heart for His selfless work on the cross. I'm so thankful for His sacrifice that I ask Him every day, "How can I be used? What can I do for You, Lord?" Perhaps writing this book and sharing my journey with you is one small way I can serve.

Leaving the past behind, I began a new walk with Christ, and I pray you will as well—no matter what stage you are in your journey. Whether you suffer with a constant pull to the fridge, have discouragement over failed weight-loss attempts, sense an empty space that you are filling with food, or you are hoping to glean motivation, this book is for you. I often receive letters from women who tell me they have lost twenty, thirty, forty, and even ninety pounds. Weight they could never lose before is finally coming off. *What's their secret to success?* It's the same as mine. We've finally moved faith to the forefront, which includes putting God first in our plan to lose weight.

As I take you with me on the journey through weight loss, I'd like us to step out of the box and step into a better understanding of our complexity. God's Word teaches that we consist of a physical body and a spirit. And yet it also speaks of our "flesh." Now our flesh in this sense doesn't refer to our actual physical flesh or skin. It refers to the innate desires or gut instincts that may be immediately satisfying but are ultimately destructive. Our physical body and spirit both play an important role in forming who we are but must be kept in line from our "flesh." If either our physical body or our spirit is out of alignment, we'll feel a spiritual imbalance.

Oftentimes we also feel a physical imbalance, which results in annoying symptoms such as a tightening waistband, lack of energy, or a disagreeable scale.

In order to recognize these separate components of your being and empower you to train them effectively, we'll discuss these three elements and how they work together throughout the pages of this book.

Starting a diet or buying a new shade of lipstick won't put you on a path to freedom. It might make you feel good on the outside, which is a natural part of your womanhood, but the change must begin with the transformation by the Spirit—the renewing of our minds.

In the next eighteen chapters, I'm going to teach you how to fill that empty space that calls out for food. I'll encourage you along the journey like a personal trainer that's cheering you on. I'll share ideas that will help you put down the food when it's time and later wisely pick it up again, and I'll offer practical tips on eating well and getting fit.

At the end of the following chapters, you'll find a section called "The Pantry: Chocked-full of Food for Thought." The pantry is organized for readers on the go, who want to flip open the book and grab something to chew on. There you'll find "A Slice of Advice," which is my response to personal fan mail. You'll also find "A Pinch of Practicality" offering practical application ideas and a quote in "The Candy Dish." And if you are looking for a recap of Scripture used in each chapter, check out "Food for Thought."

In a recent interview with *US Weekly* magazine, I was asked, "You're not starving yourself, right?"

The truth is that I love to eat, and I don't mind putting out the energy to stay fit. I enjoy wine with dinner, and I love my dessert, but the difference is that I've become accustomed to making better choices in the *way* I eat. Do I count calories? Not a chance. Do I make good choices with faith-focused determination? Absolutely!

Finally getting it right, I'm twenty-five pounds lighter than I was on *Full House*, I have a full house of my own, and I feel better than I ever did!

TWO

The Inside Scoop

While many of you were enjoying the summer heat by the pool, I was enjoying an early Christmas in Chester, Vermont, filming the Hallmark movie *Moonlight & Mistletoe*, where I starred alongside the adorable Tom Arnold.

Once the movie was wrapped, I answered the usual questions like:

- What is Tom Arnold like?
- What is an average day like when you're working on set?
- Can you tell us about your wardrobe?
- How did they keep the snow from melting?
- Did you pick up any makeup tips that you can use at home?
- Do you have any upcoming projects in the works?

I can tell you that most days started around 7:00 a.m. and we shot twelve to fourteen hour days. Some days were really hot, which was difficult when you have on five layers of T-shirts, sweaters, coats, gloves, and scarves! I was pretty much in every scene so there wasn't a day I didn't work. And after my long day was done, I'd have another hour of work back in my hotel room learning the next day's lines. That was an average day.

I can also tell you that Tom Arnold was wonderful to work with; I loved watching him work. His creativity in delivering everyday lines is inspiring! He was generous on the set, buying the crew ice cream and pizzas on long days, and he respected my faith.

In this chapter I'm going to give you the inside scoop, but it won't be about television, movies, or magazines. This one will be about *you*. When we fully understand what is really going on inside us, we can then understand *why* we're inclined to make the choices we do. We'll also understand why the transforming of our bodies must begin by the renewing of our minds. Our bodies aren't making these detrimental choices for us; they are simply animated by a mind that needs a mental makeover. Let's get started, shall we?

Breaking Up Is Hard to Do

Changing our thought pattern sounds like a step we can easily take, but the problem we often find ourselves facing is that our minds are in one place while our heart is in another. Since we're so in love with food, the thought of breaking up with it is devastating. Just remember, it's only food; it's not like you're going to prom together. And I don't know about you, but I'd rather go alone than with an extra twenty pounds around my waist. Been there, done that! Yeah, I know we're not supposed to feel self-conscious about such things, but it's hard not to feel a little "Ugly Betty," when you're under the microscope on national television. Wearing an off-the-shoulder, puffy-sleeved green velvet dress, while my half-sized television rival had on a slinky little black one, I watched my date kissing his ex. While DJ made her entrance on stage that night, I wanted nothing more than to make a quick exit, put on a baggy sweatshirt, and call it a night. Who did I turn to for comfort? Most likely food, since we were in a steady relationship at the time.

As a result of this mind-set, many of us spend our lifetime searching for a miraculous way to keep the binge and lose the bulge. Instead of taming our uncontrolled appetite to behave like it should, we continue to nurture and spoil it over time. The morning starts off with a longing for lunch and a yearning for "just the right thing," till we get it. We complain how bloated we feel after lunch, and then within an hour we're back to discussing what dinner will be. The cycle continues until it ends somewhere around 11:00 p.m. with another snack on our lap. *Sound familiar?*

One problem with our overweight society is that we've been trained to look at food as the problem rather than our approach to appetite. Food has become the focus of our culture with fast-food signs adorning every street corner. In hopes of fixing this obsession with food, we find diet plans that offer twice the binge at half the calories, or we reach for pills that will quickly shed the pounds. Sounds great when one finds out that she can still eat till her eyes are leaking and not gain a pound, but what she isn't learning in the process is how to behave as a disciplined eater, or that God calls us to *moderation* in all things.

He doesn't say, "Eat this; avoid that," or, "Hey, girl, have you counted the calories in that bagel?" He wisely instructs us to be moderate. First Timothy 4:4–5 says, "For everything God created is good, and nothing is to be rejected if it is received with thanksgiving, because it is consecrated by the word of God and prayer."

Diets usually fail for one or all of these three reasons:

1. **No Pain No Gain.** We choose to sprint instead of training for the long run.
2. **We're Spoiled.** We try to change only the food that we eat instead of changing our mind-set.
3. **Lack of Conviction.** We don't truly believe that the benefits are worth the effort it takes to get us there.

Which one are you?

Reason 1: No Pain No Gain

"No discipline seems pleasant at the time, but painful. Later on, however, it produces a harvest of righteousness and peace for those who have been trained by it" (Heb. 12:11)

What shape is your resistance muscle in? Has it been lying dormant for years? If so, I imagine that any workout, big or small, results in discomfort and pain.

Training and discipline are so important to achieving success. Without discipline we'll run for a bit but tire out long before the race is won. We might pick it up again in six months to a year and do the entire sprint over again with the same result.

If we want permanent solutions, we have to train ourselves for the long run. Since my husband Val played for the NHL, I have seen the vigorous training regimen he's had to go through. Val knows that in order to play the game and to play it well, which he does, it's going to take training and conviction on his part. It's not about the way he *feels* at the moment; it's what he *must do* to win.

An important aspect in training is that of our muscle memory. Muscle memory involves the repetition of skills until the movements become automatic. Many of us use the muscle memory for simple things like tying a shoe or brushing our teeth. The movements have been so repetitious over the years that we now do them without thought. Hey, I even find myself tying my kid's shoes without thought!

In the same way I had to train my resistance muscles in the beginning by saying "No" more often than "Yes." By repeating the exercise of discipline, I have formulated a lifestyle change.

Let's be careful not to confuse this exercise with deprivation. It's okay to have dessert, even if it's a double-decker, chocolate-chip brownie drenched in caramel sauce; but it's best to enjoy such things in moderation rather than daily. My rule of thumb for special treats is once or twice a week. It's good to resist, but let's not get extreme.

I've also trained my thoughts to accept wholesome food as the norm rather than reaching for fast or fried food. Though it wasn't always that way. I was a girl whose mom took her to McDonald's for a quarter pounder and fries before every audition. But the more I consciously made an effort to choose healthier foods, the more I unconsciously became accustomed to them. Now these foods are naturally my first choice.

Exercise is equally important to me as my diet is, but the only reason these changes became a permanent part of my lifestyle is because my thoughts were trained to accept them as *necessary* rather than *optional*.

Reason 2: We're Spoiled

The other night I made chicken and salad for dinner—or maybe it was pasta. I don't exactly recall what we all had, but I do remember Maks liking it all a little too much! When Maks likes what he's eating (which is often the case), he just keeps on scooping it in until I notice his sweet little cheeks getting full, and I say, "Maks, honey, you've had enough." It's a good thing I'm there to monitor him since I fear the little guy may one day explode.

After dinner he started in on dessert, taking an apple, followed by a banana, along with high hopes of having yet another apple or two—until I stopped him again. You don't want to be the person behind him at an all-you-can-eat-buffet; trust me on that.

Finally it was time to put the kids into bed. Lev was brushing his teeth, Natasha was reading a book, and Maks was parading around the room tapping on his little round belly.

"Uh, Mom?" he said, finally pausing for breath. "There may be a problem. I think I'm pregnant!"

Lines like that aren't written in Hollywood; they're birthed in those quiet moments we pause long enough to breathe in the wonderful world around us. I had to pause for a breath myself while I stifled a laugh before explaining to him that he wasn't about to give me a grandkid or by the looks of it, two.

I also found it a good time to explain that we don't have to go hog wild when we're eating just because it tastes good. We need to consider what's best for our bodies, when to say, "When." It's my job as a mom to train him until he's equipped to make that decision himself.

In much the same way many untrained adults eat as they please because they aren't trained to consider the result of their actions. They see where their actions have gotten them but don't realize the difference discipline would have made.

One might say something like, "Overeating this *once* isn't such a big deal. I can eat this, that, and the other; then I'll just get back on track in the morning!" Getting on track is important, but the plan often falls through because we've started allowing sloppy habits to form. I don't let my kids get away with such behavior, so why would I condone it for myself?

Spoiled eaters have never learned to control their appetite and choose to focus on the food instead of their lust for it. Their diet may consist of a day at the trough munching on countless low-cal alternatives instead of seeing the real problem at hand—volume. This line may sound familiar, "I can eat all the carrots and celery sticks that I want!"

My question is, "Why would you eat all the carrots you want? Shouldn't we just eat all the carrots we need?"

Once spoiled eaters tire of the tasteless "all-you-can-squeeze-in" buffet, the high-calorie foods sneak back in one by one. Finally they wonder why diets don't work.

Spoiled eaters seek out quick-fix diets that promise a lot in return for a little.

Reason 3: Lack of Conviction

The unconvicted mind is destined for failure because when the going gets tough—and it will—they don't have a good enough reason to stick to the plan. Unconvicted eaters often find themselves hosting debates in their minds with food as the ultimate prize. They pepper their thoughts with persuasive arguments like, "I'm already thirty-something; maybe it's time I accepted the fact that overweight is okay for me." Or, "I'm doing so much work just so I can be twenty pounds lighter. It's not like I'll be prettier or anything." And, "I have my whole life to take off the weight; why worry about it tonight?"

All of those arguments may be worth consideration, but they should never be considered while in the throes of a late-night craving feast. A little soul searching at the *start* of the journey is a good time to discover the reasons you want to lose weight. I suggest jotting them down on a piece of paper so you can pull them out for a read when you get that sudden urge to bolt. (Better yet, review the list daily as a constant reminder.)

That internal argument is familiar to most of us, but do most of us recognize what it is? It's our flesh and our spirit fighting to lead. Our flesh is ruled by passion and desire, but our spirit is led by wisdom and truth.

"So I say, live by the Spirit, and you will not gratify the desires of the sinful nature." (Gal. 5:16)

Training my thoughts to yield to the Spirit is an exercise I do minute by minute and will continue to do throughout life. I wasn't always sure which argument it held, but it gets easier to discern over time. Now I understand the consequences of my actions, and I'm led by conviction.

Just last night around 10:00 p.m. my stomach started growling. It had been about three hours since dinner, so in good conscience I could have had a light snack. But knowing that I was going to bed within thirty minutes, I decided to fight my flesh, which desperately wanted a sweet treat, and yield to my spirit that told me, "You don't need a scone right before bed. Wait and have a good breakfast in the morning. You know you'll feel better about it tomorrow."

And you know what? I did feel much better about it this morning. Learn to remind yourself, "If I overeat today, I'll weaken my resistance muscle, which I've worked diligently to build up. I want to finally take the weight off this year, so I'll keep pressing on."

This is an exercise we should apply to all areas of our lives, which I'll also suggest with many of the other lessons in this book. It's my desire that you find freedom through weight loss—no one should be trapped in a body controlled by their appetite—but first and foremost I pray that you find this freedom through faith.

What is your conviction? If you're not sure, it's important that you do a little soul searching to find it. Do you desire to lose a few pounds—to lose a lot more than a few? If you do, then consider the "why?" When we're able to answer that question, we can then apply a solution that works!

The Pantry
CHOCKED-FULL OF FOOD FOR THOUGHT

The Main Ingredient

There are many wonderful weight-loss plans out there for us to choose from. In fact it's easy to find one that's a fit for our lifestyle and health. The basic plan I suggest is to stop abusing yourself with food, start making healthier choices, and get serious with God. Move more, control your portions, make wise choices, and keep God close by your side. Stick to that plan, and you'll see some results!

A Slice of Advice

Dear Candace,

I read the article about you in the December issue of Us Weekly *magazine. What really caught my eye was the amount of weight you have lost since* Full House *ended! For a small person like you, twenty-two pounds is a lot of weight.*

Throughout my adult life my weight has literally been a yo-yo, up one year then down the next. Every time I lose a substantial amount of weight I manage to gain most of it back within about a two-year period; then I have to start all over again. At fifty-two years old I can't keep on doing that all the time.

For whatever reason, I have not been able to maintain my weight once I lose it. I do know what I have to do. My question to you is, how can I maintain this weight loss?

I know that I have to exercise, and I have started walking after dinner. My problem is that once I lose the desired weight, I go back to eating.

Once I treat myself to something, I can't get back on track. I would really appreciate it if you could share some of your secrets. I really need to hear from someone who has had success not only in losing but also in keeping the weight off.
—Michelle

Dear Michelle,

Weight loss is difficult, and keeping it off can be even harder! Obviously, you know how to get it off—diet and exercise. Eating the right foods is key, and staying on top of exercise is equally important. Your changes need to be a way of life. It's okay to have a dessert here and there or a side of fries once in a while, but bringing those foods back into your daily diet will cause you to gain weight back and possibly more, as you already know.

I make sure that if I'm going to indulge in some goodies, I do it moderately, then I'm back to my wholesome diet. I'm conscience of what I put into my mouth every day although I'm not obsessive about it, which can be just as dangerous.

Honestly, because I've been eating healthy, fresh foods for so long, eating things fried or processed make my body feel bad. It may give me a headache or make me feel tired or even sick. I don't like feeling that way, while knowing I can feel better just by the foods I'm eating.

If you know that it's dangerous for you to eat your favorite unhealthy foods just once, then cut them out completely. I know for some people, it's all or nothing. If that's you, then refrain from eating all unhealthy foods. If however, you can exhibit self-control and eat sweets in moderation, I would recommend this method. The latter works for me as denying myself ALL sugar would make me go crazy! I prefer knowing I can have it, but choose not to, except on occasion. That is the exercise of my fruit of the spirit (self-control)!

I encourage you to wisely keep the mental aspect of eating and exercising in line with God's Word.

Renewing your mind each and every day through prayer and reading the Bible can help you get a grip on not going back to your old habits. Commit to keeping your body a holy temple. God can give you the strength to do it. It will shine inside and out when you put the right things into it.
—Candace

A Pinch of Practicality

Read Romans 7 in order to gain a better understanding of Paul's struggle in the flesh. Listen to how he compares it to the freedom found in chapter 8. Paul wrote those chapters so brilliantly, illustrating how one is the solution to the other.

Start strength training by making wise choices that exercise your resistance muscle.

Ways to strengthen your resistance may include:

- Passing on the junk food aisle in the grocery store.
- Making a healthy choice when eating out.
- Passing on the goodies at group meetings.
- Taking one trip to a buffet instead of two or more.
- Eating until you're satisfied rather than stuffed.
- Limiting treats to once or twice a week rather than daily.

Set aside some quiet time to write a letter to yourself. Let God in on this too. It may take one letter; it may take a few. Prayerfully consider the changes you'd like to see in your life and the reasons you'd like to see change. This letter is for your eyes only, so feel free to hide it or tear it up later. The important exercise here is that you decide what is good and why it's important to you before you continue this journey.

Food for Thought

The following list is a recap of the Scriptures we covered in this chapter. You may find it helpful to post them around the house on little notes where you'll see them often. The Bible is great encouragement for every step of the way:

- For everything God created is good, and nothing is to be rejected if it is received with thanksgiving, because it is consecrated by the word of God and prayer. (1 Tim. 4:4–5 NIV)
- No discipline seems pleasant at the time, but painful. Later on, however, it produces a harvest of righteousness and peace for those who have been trained by it. (Heb. 12:11 NIV)
- So I say, live by the Spirit, and you will not gratify the desires of the sinful nature. (Gal. 5:16 NIV)

The Candy Dish

Excellence is an art won by training and habituation. We do not act rightly because we have virtue or excellence, but we rather have those because we have acted rightly. We are what we repeatedly do. Excellence, then, is not an act but a habit. —Aristotle

Easy Chicken Noodle Soup

INGREDIENTS

8 small carrots chopped

4 cups chicken broth

2 cups water

1 clove garlic, pierced with a toothpick

12 ounces boneless, skinless chicken breast

⅓ cup, packed parsley

2 cups dry egg noodles (fine)

2 teaspoons lemon juice

Salt and freshly ground black pepper

DIRECTIONS

Combine carrots, chicken broth, water, and garlic in a large pot. Cover and bring to a boil. Reduce heat to medium, and simmer until the carrots are tender, about five minutes.

While that is cooking, cut the chicken. I cut it into half-inch chunks. Rinse them, pat dry with a paper towel, and mince the parsley.

Add the chicken and egg noodles to the broth; cover and cook until the chicken is cooked through (about 5 minutes).

Stir in the lemon juice and parsley. Fish out garlic clove and season to taste with salt and pepper.

THREE

Grab Wings and Soar

Reshaping it all has been a lifelong journey, which started the moment I took my first breath. Born on April 6, 1976, in Panorama City, California, to Robert and Barbara Cameron, I entered the world as Candace Helaine Cameron. I was the youngest sister to three siblings, my brother Kirk and two sisters, Bridgette and Melissa. Dad was a public middle-school teacher, while Mom's job was a stay-at-home role that ensured our faces were clean, our tummies were full, and clean underwear was ready when we were.

Being the youngest of four, I enjoyed special times with my mom. After the other kids left for school, we'd pick up some apple fritters and take on the day. I was her traveling companion, and together we had a lot of traveling to do: dropping clothes at the cleaners, picking up groceries, putting gas in the car, and finally picking up my brother and sisters from school again.

When Mom wasn't in the car, she was at the house, doing her best to make it a home. She made the most incredible spaghetti known to mankind, using a blend of tomato sauces, as well as both stewed and diced tomatoes. It was meaty and rich with ground beef and Italian sausage, served with garlic French bread on the side. Stepping through the front door on spaghetti night is one smell I will never forget.

With Mom around we never went hungry. Dinner was always on the table, which was often fish and rice or chicken with mashed potatoes, and veggies on the side. Peas, corn, and carrots were regular visitors to my plate.

It was also our thing to have turkey tacos four or five days a week. We loved them, and since they were easy to make, Mom made them a lot. It became a staple in our house that we all learned to make; in fact they're so simple that I often make them for my kids too. She could have used ground beef but Mom knew turkey was a leaner choice that tasted similar to beef, and was better for us. It does have a lighter taste, but once seasoned there is not a big difference. We loved them then and still do.

I loved watching Mom in the kitchen. Her long blonde ponytail would sway as she moved, and her smile told me she loved being there. I loved being there too, knowing I was Mom's helper when the kids were at school. Being a helper meant I got to taste everything too, which is probably the reason I hung out so much in the kitchen at all.

When I think of my dad, I fondly remember white T-shirts, along with his worn-out jeans that were stained with grease spots and paint blops. Those stains served to remind us that Dad could and would fix everything. He was the ultimate handyman, who put his skills to use on the house. They always lived in the same place, but over the years the house has gone through several major remodeling jobs, including the time our garage was transformed into a family room. Dad would hire out for some jobs, but any job he could do himself, he would. He drove a light-blue Volkswagen Beetle to work every day, and left the Volkswagen van for Mom and us kids. Because of his rugged, handsome looks and wavy brown hair, he was often compared to Michael Landon.

Dad came from a background of healthy eating, while Mom was the opposite. She was brought up in a home that when they ate cold cereal in the morning, they needed to add two tablespoons of sugar to sweeten it up. At times it felt like a battleground when deciding on the type of food and what we could eat. Mom wasn't deliberately unhealthy; she just wasn't as health conscious as Dad, who often tried to implement healthy alternatives.

Our eating habits changed from year to year. For several years we were on the Pritikin Diet, which is based on a book by Nathan Pritikin. The diet is based on vegetables, grains, and fruit. It wasn't strictly vegetarian, but it did have a low percentage of fat. Basically it tasted like cardboard. Dad taught us healthier ways to eat, but they weren't great-tasting options. At the same time Mom would buy chips for our lunch boxes, take us out for fast food, and keep a healthy supply of ice cream in our freezer. Her options weren't so healthy but tasted incredibly good. She tried her best to respect Dad's efforts, but because she loved the naughty but nice food, she'd sneak it into the house.

I started to view food in either one of two ways—it was either delicious but forbidden, or it was acceptable and tasteless. The bottom line is that I was left confused. I really believe that this confusion set the stage for the bad eating habits I had throughout my teen years and into early adulthood. Without clear direction and understanding we're bound to face failure.

A double minded man is unstable in all his ways. (James 1:8 KJV)

Dad wouldn't allow soda, so drinking water was something he encouraged a lot. Depending on the year my mom would have Diet Pepsi in the fridge, but that was the forbidden fruit we dare not touch. Thankfully I acquired a taste for water; in fact I love it, and it's still the first drink I reach for today.

When I was five, things started to get busy for Mom. She was running Kirk, Melissa, and me to auditions in LA. Dad's schedule worked out perfectly. He was home by 3:30, so if Mom was busy driving one kid, he could watch the other three and help out with homework.

I knew the routine. I would come out of the school, and if Mom was parked at the start of the pickup line, then I knew that I had an audition. If that was the case, we'd leave right away and head over the hill to the west side. She would have my clothes clean, pressed, and ready to go so I could change in the car. I didn't wear fancy dresses of any kind, but I did have a few outfits that were my audition clothes. I had three pairs of OshKosh overalls, one purple, one turquoise blue, and the other denim, which I rolled up twice for a cuff. A white T-shirt and pink Converse high tops finished the look. Mom thought that bright colors helped me look cute and hip. I suppose that I did look hip back then, but times have definitely changed. She also packed a butane curling iron so she could throw a few curls in my hair and put it in pigtails or a side ponytail. Unlike pageants, which I've never been in, makeup was a definite no no for auditions. I had to look cute, fresh, and natural.

Most days I was excited, but as the years progressed, or if the day was tiring, I'd be bummed out knowing that we had a long drive ahead. That's where McDonalds came in. It was well worth the drive if I knew a quarter-pounder, fries, and a drink were in it for me. Even when I was just six or seven, a Happy Meal didn't suffice. That little burger was far too small.

I don't know how she ever found the time to teach me how to ride a bike, but she did. I remember climbing up on top of it while she held the back steady. There was an incline on our street that looked like a mountain at the time, but when I look at it now, I see it's barely a hill. After holding on to the back for two or three days, she knew I was ready to take off on my own.

"Don't let go!" I said. But when we got to the top of the hill, she did. I didn't know it at first, but when I found out that I was riding alone, I was thrilled! It was smooth sailing from that moment on; I finally had wings to soar.

Laser tag, hide-and-seek, and bike riding kept us busy on the street. I didn't play any team sports, but we were always active nonetheless.

I was a regular-sized kid until about the age of nine. I wasn't big, and I wasn't small. When I hit nine years old, the chipmunk cheeks set in. It was probably a combination of exercising less, being that I was in school full-time, and eating more junk since I was exposed to more food. I played jump rope at recess but didn't get involved in vigorous games like kick ball or tag, and when lunch came around, it was a tempting new world. We had healthy lunches packed for us, but unfortunately those lunches were dull. While I ate cardboard, my friends feasted on Ding Dongs, Ho Hos, and cake. So like Michael Douglas in *Wall Street*, I became a master trader who managed to get my hands on their stock.

I also started taking trips to the corner store with my friends. Soon enough, Pixie Stix, Fun Dip, and Big League Chewing gum were in a serious relationship with my tongue. I preferred sugar to salt and still do to this day.

I don't think my parents realized just how much access I had to junk. They were doing their best to keep our diet focused on health while I was finding ways to sneak in a snack.

Our family wasn't the only ones with a health-conscious attitude. Our friends Ryan and Andrew lived much the same way, and since our parents were best friends, we were together all the time. In the winter we spent almost every weekend with them, and in the summer it was almost every day. Health wasn't the only thing we had in common: my dad did gymnastics in high school and college, and their dad did too. He was an acrobat in the circus; their mom was too. In fact, after being a trapeze artist, she went on to be Tinkerbelle at Disneyland. Hooked up to a harness and cable, five foot tall Patty would descend from the Matterhorn, flying across the park with her wand.

By the time I was ten, my all-too-famous chubby little cheeks had set in. I wasn't large, but I definitely wasn't thin either, and it was starting to show. That summer my sisters and I hit the park a little more often with Ryan and Andrew, which gave me some exercise. I was also away from the Ding Dongs at school. When I came back for the second season of *Full House*, I had lost five of those pounds, got a curly new perm, and had grown a bit taller. I was aware of my body, but at eleven-years-old I wasn't obsessing.

I remember Gina the costume designer saying, "Wow you grew; you look great!" In a sensitive way she encouraged me.

I felt confident and pretty that year. I got that spiral perm at a salon in the valley where my brother and dad got their hair done as well. Mom had a few perms of her own, which was probably what spurred us on to get mine done too. My hair was almost to my waist by then, and so with the weight of my hair, they were able to give me a tight curl. It was the 1980s—Linda Ronstadt, Whitney Houston, and Madonna had big hair—I wanted it too!

Before the perm Mom spent a lot of time curling my hair before bed. She liked to see my hair curled for auditions and special occasions. We used soft pink spongy rollers, which would hold the curl the entire next day. They were uncomfortable, but I got used to sleeping in them after a while. If we ever lost those rollers (and in a house with six people, we seemed to lose everything), she would use socks that doubled as rag curlers. Wrapping my hair around the sock, she tied each into a bow. They now sell long spongy tubes that do the job, but we didn't have those back then, so I went to bed with a head full of socks.

Our careers were a lot of work on Mom's part, but she did it because she saw both the fun and the potential we had. She didn't intend for any of us to be actors; in fact her friend talked her into letting us take the plunge into acting. But once we started acting and doing it so well, we were excited and knew it was something we wanted to pursue.

Our parents were upfront about giving us the option to leave. At age seven, after just one commercial, Melissa took that option. I think the process scared her to death. Life has a way of doing that to us. It can seem so alluring at times as we embark on new projects, but once we're involved in the process, we discover that reaching the finish line might take some tears and some sweat.

I was blessed with my share of tears too. An even greater blessing was having a mom whose arms were always open to me and who was ready with a listening ear. I remember running into those arms when I was about thirteen years old. I was suffering from a serious addiction at the time—Kool-Aid. In those days the thing to do was to buy packets of presweetened Kool-Aid, fill up a baggy and lick to your heart's content. Most kids had a stash at home they could dig into, but I had to hide mine in a backpack or keep the canister at school. It was kind of gross actually when you consider that I dipped my finger into the bag and licked it repeatedly throughout the day.

Gross wasn't my concern at the time; the sugar rush was. After several weeks of doing this, the daily sugar crash took its toll on me until finally I broke down, crying in Mom's arms. I was unhappy with how I felt and, at the tender age of thirteen, also with how I looked. I wanted and needed a change.

Mom has struggled with weight her entire life. It's always been a battle for her to fight the draw toward the food she loves. Bridgette and Melissa were older than me, and both of them had a few pounds to lose. Collectively we decided to join a popular weight-loss plan, which involved prepackaged dehydrated meals, much like astronaut food to me. I didn't really like adding water to dehydrated food or watching it come to life in the microwave, but it taught me portion control. Bridgette responded well to the diet and got the most out of it. Like I always say, different methods of weight loss work for different people, but this particular one wasn't working for me.

As I take you through this book, my hope is to encourage you to get off the fence, find healthy but satisfying ways to take off the weight, and build on a firm foundation that you can stand on for life. I'll hang on to the back of your bike for a while, but soon you'll be riding alone. There is a place of freedom, when the trying just becomes living. It becomes smooth sailing from that moment on, when you finally have wings to soar.

> *Therefore everyone who hears these words of mine and puts them into practice is like a wise man who built his house on the rock. The rain came down, the streams rose, and the winds blew and beat against that house; yet it did not fall, because it had its foundation on the rock. (Matt. 7:24–25)*

The Pantry
CHOCKED-FULL OF FOOD FOR THOUGHT

The Main Ingredient

Confusion about our bodies and our health only leads to ongoing frustration. We need to stop the cycle of yoyo dieting and settle on a healthy way to live. There is a better alternative than tasteless yet healthy food. And there's also a better alternative to a diet filled with fast food and sugary treats. It's delicious food that works to the benefit of our bodies. With a deeper understanding of what works to our benefit, we increase our chance at success.

A Slice of Advice

Dear Candace,

I've seen photos of your family, and you're all beautiful. Your daughter is looking like a miniature you. So cute! You all look so radiant it's amazing. I read somewhere online (maybe Twitter?) that your children love sushi. I couldn't believe it because I can barely get mine to like tuna.

I want to train my children to eat healthier food. I try to eliminate sugary sweats and oversweetened cereals as much as I can, but my husband and I are at a constant battle on this one. He thinks that if we deprive them of good food they will just want it all the more. Any advice you can give us?

—Janelle

Dear Janelle,

Thanks for your kind words. I think my kids are radiant too! Hopefully it's a bit of the Lord shining through, but I do believe it's also because of what they are eating.

I think your husband is viewing healthy food as the enemy, so maybe you can help him discover tasty choices that are good for us too. I encourage you to try some of the recipes in this book and experiment a little on your own to offer some good alternatives.

Treats aren't the enemy either. It's okay to have them occasionally and in moderation. But keep a close eye so they don't overindulge. Just like us their hearts need to be trained to listen to their heads, but for now they're listening to you for that guidance. So grab the opportunity to guide them well.

There's nothing wrong with rules. In fact many rules are there to save our lives, but telling someone to live according to them and giving them a reason to live that way are two entirely different things. One is preaching; the other is teaching. Set healthy boundaries for them, and let them know why you are doing it.

They might not appreciate having to eat asparagus as a side dish, but encourage them to have a bite. Who knows—they might like it! Get them to try it again the next time you make it because their taste buds are continually changing.

Hope that helps!

—Candace

A Pinch of Practicality

Eating good food is one thing. Dining well is another. On the next page are five practical tips for eating that will help you slow down and improve your dining experience:

1. Eye your food first. Does it look like too much? Decide on a smaller portion and stay with your choice unless you find you're not satisfied. You can always go back for a little bit more if need be.
2. Use smaller plates. Smaller plates give us the illusion of larger portions, and larger portions convince us we're satisfied. Our ancestors ate off dishes that are much smaller than we have become accustomed to.
3. Have a glass of cold water with your meal and take sips often. Drinking water will help you slow down and enjoy your food.
4. Engage in conversation if you are dining with others. The fellowship is equally as important as the food, so sit back and listen between bites. Don't worry, your plate isn't leaving.
5. Chew your food slowly. The longer you take to eat a meal, the less food you will consume. And by eating slower, you will also savor the flavor.

Food for Thought

- A double minded man is unstable in all his ways. (James 1:8 KJV)
- Therefore everyone who hears these words of mine and puts them into practice is like a wise man who built his house on the rock. The rain came down, the streams rose, and the winds blew and beat against that house; yet it did not fall, because it had its foundation on the rock. (Matt. 7:24–25)

The Candy Dish

People who soar are those who refuse to sit back, sigh and wish things would change. They neither complain of their lot nor

passively dream of some distant ship coming in. Rather, they visualize in their minds that they are not quitters; they will not allow life's circumstances to push them down and hold them under.
—Charles R. Swindoll

From My Stove to Yours

Turkey Tacos

Serves 4

INGREDIENTS

  1 pound ground turkey (or lean beef)
  1 15½ ounce can black beans, drained and rinsed
  1 package flour or corn tortillas
  Lettuce, shredded
  Tomatoes, diced
  1 bag of shredded cheddar or Mexican cheese blend

DIRECTIONS

Brown the ground turkey or beef in a pan over medium heat until cooked through.

  Heat beans as directed.

  Add a scoop of meat to a warmed tortilla. Add beans or place them on the side. Serve with shredded lettuce, tomatoes, cheese, and fresh salsa.

Top with fresh salsa:
  1 diced tomato
  Chopped purple onion, to taste
  Chopped cilantro, to taste
  Salt and pepper

FOUR

Dad's Infinity and Beyond

One of the perks of acting at such a young age is that I earned a tremendous amount of money for such a young person growing up. You'd have thought that a girl in my position would have been living in the lap of luxury, wearing the best fashion money could buy and driving the finest of cars, but Dad had other plans for my life.

My father earned his living teaching public middle school, math and physical education, while raising a family of six. He believed people should work hard for the things they have, and so he instilled that idea in us. He could see that hard work was not only a prerequisite for success but that it was also a prerequisite for strong character. Struggling for the things we get teaches us the all-important lesson of self-discipline while it strengthens our body and spirit. It wasn't enough for us to achieve a level of success in this world; our parents wanted us to reach our full potential as people who are strong in spirit and mind.

Although my brother Kirk and I were in a position to do it, Dad wasn't comfortable with the idea of any sixteen-year-old blowing truckloads of cash. The success of *Full House* and *Growing Pains* was phenomenal, but that wasn't about to change the dynamics of our all-American family. Maintaining a level of normalcy at home was also important. Whether I appeared on the cover of *Brio* magazine, or walked the red carpet that day, behind closed doors we were a family living much like everyone else. I still squabbled with my sisters when washing the dishes and waited in line for the bathroom in a house with three siblings. My rise to success didn't change the atmosphere of our family or offer me a free pass from hard work.

Buying my first car was a bit of a battle. Knowing how much I enjoyed acting, Dad didn't think of it as "earning" in the sense of hard work. I enjoyed being on the set every day and loved acting, so it wasn't as though I was working in a busy supermarket dealing with angry customers, crying babies, and cleanups on aisle four. He knew it was income, but he still wanted me to learn the value of setting a goal, counting the cost, weighing the gain, and doing the legwork it takes in reaching that goal. It was time to sit down and formulate a plan.

Taking a part-time job at a restaurant wasn't an option for me, so we got a little creative. During the height of the success of *Full House*, I was asked to attend massive events nationwide where I did autograph signings and public appearances mainly at shopping malls or civic arenas. These events weren't nearly as glamorous for me as you'd think and were particularly exhausting. Although it was great to meet my fans, trying to sign posters and take photos with up to twenty-five thousand people at an event could get seriously overwhelming. But income from those events and sales from merchandise allowed me that additional hard-earned money. My dad agreed that once I had enough money earned from those weekends, I could purchase the car, so I got to work. After several months a black Nissan Pathfinder rolled off the lot and into my life. I loved that SUV!

About a year or two later the same dealership had a great price on an Infiniti Q45, a luxury sedan that my dad had his eye on but couldn't afford. I knew without a doubt that I wanted to buy it for him, and after talking it over with Mom, she agreed to let me.

I never considered it a gift from me. Since I was part of a family, it was from all of us kids, the way I knew it should be. Together we wrapped the car in a large red ribbon, tucked it into the garage, and waited for Dad to get back from school.

It was an emotional moment for all of us when the door finally opened and we looked at his face. Humble and grateful, the tears stung his eyes. My parents chose to live a life as normal as they possibly could so that we might learn the value of setting and reaching a goal. We learned that a goal itself is not to be desired but rather that value is found in the effort.

By learning the hard way, Dad taught me five important steps in reaching my goals:

1. Envision your goal.
2. Formulate a plan.
3. Consider the gain.
4. Count the cost.
5. Do the necessary work to achieve it.

Both planning our goals and the means of getting there gives us a greater chance at success than living impulsively would. When things are organized and on schedule, the likelihood of success is increased. Unexpected obstacles often stand in our way, but if we invest in foresight and consider the ways we will deal with each hurdle, we are leaning on wisdom rather than chance.

In *The Ultimate Weight Solution: The 7 Keys to Weight Loss Freedom*, Dr. Phil McGraw writes,

> *Because I have counseled so many overweight patients, I can tell you with absolute certainty why some people stay fit and others do not. If someone is successful in keeping weight off for five, ten, twenty, or more years, they have carefully planned thoughtful goals that they hold to and live by.*[1]

The Bible also reminds us to consider carefully our plans before we set out to build: "Suppose one of you wants to build a tower. Will he not first sit down and estimate the cost to see if he has enough money to complete it? For if he lays the foundation and is not able to finish it, everyone who sees it will ridicule him, saying, 'This fellow began to build and was not able to finish'" (Luke 14:28–30).

In that passage Jesus was pointing out the cost of being a disciple. Life will offer us a thousand and one reasons we shouldn't follow Christ, but those who have built their faith on conviction won't give up because they have counted the cost beforehand and their eyes are fixed on the goal ahead. The same principle should apply to the important life goals we set. We consider the pros and cons *before* we start; then we map out a reasonable plan and stick to it.

The empowering words "first sit down and estimate the cost" can revitalize any life when we put them in action. If we've mapped out a solid plan, we have a healthy chance of reaching the goal, and of course success will also depend on whether you're doing all that you humanly can to adhere to the rules. Human effort is all that's ever expected of us, and it's all we should ever expect from ourselves.

Do you have a recipe for success? Have you carefully considered your weight-loss goal and detailed the means you'll take in getting there? If you haven't taken that important step, I urge you to grab a pen and paper—a pretty little journal if you have one—and answer the three following questions in detail:

1. What is the goal you hope to attain? (Weight loss, better health, release from the bondage of food, more energy, a fitness routine, etc.) Without a specific goal in mind, it's nearly impossible to attain it. Be specific. If you want to lose weight, decide how much you hope to lose and when you hope to reach this goal. Knowing how much you want to lose will be the measuring stick to the time and effort required to lose the extra pounds. It will also measure the lifestyle changes required in maintaining the loss.

2. What do you hope to gain by reaching this goal? (I'll feel younger, gain respect, feel accepted, look beautiful, etc.) Answer honestly; and don't worry, no one but you will peek at your answer. By looking at the emotion behind the goal, you may also discover your drive. Hopefully this step of self-analysis will give you a deeper understanding of yourself. It could prompt you to choose a direction you've never considered before. If the answer is "to be skinny," then go one step further and ask what being skinny would mean to you. Our reasons tend to shift over time, and therefore it's an interesting exercise to evaluate where you are today.

3. What is the cost? What is it going to take to make this change? Will you do the legwork it takes to reach this goal? If you want to lose weight, carefully map out the plan, listing the life changes you'll make to get you there. If drinking more water is important, then also list it here. If you want more energy, you will need to be eating well and exercising regularly. Be specific, listing things you need to eliminate as well as changes you need to incorporate. It might be that you

are taking things slow, making one change per week, or it could be that you need to make several changes now.

The ability to envision your goal and the means of getting there brings us that much closer to achieving it. We become travelers on a journey equipped with a compass and a map.

Once you have decided exactly what your final goal will be, we can start breaking it down into smaller attainable pieces. For example, if you want to lose fifty pounds this year (let's round that off to fifty-two pounds in fifty-two weeks), we can do the math and conclude that your focus for each week will be one pound. That's it—one pound per week! One hundred pounds? Then you're looking at roughly two pounds per week, which is attainable if you have counted the cost and are willing to adhere to the plan.

Author Mark Twain said, "The secret of getting ahead is getting started. The secret of getting started is breaking your complex overwhelming tasks into small manageable ones then starting on the first one."

You start by taking the first step today and concentrating on each step as it comes. If you can make it through one day, you have the same ability to make it through each day that follows. Standing face-to-face with a mountain can be overwhelming, especially when your perspective is that of looking up from the bottom. But if we decide to take one step and then another, looking only at the ground set before us, we realize the potential we have.

> Therefore do not worry about tomorrow, for tomorrow will worry about itself. Each day has enough trouble of its own. (Matt. 6:34)

Too often dieters will say, "I want to lose weight so I'll start cutting back." And that's pretty much the end of the plan, as undefined as it may be. Be prepared for the Achilles' heel of internal negotiation. If my best friend Dilini shows up with a box of chocolates for me tonight, that I mindlessly munch while watching TV, "cutting back" may not hold the same definition that it held yesterday. If I have to start dealing with internal conflict between my desire and my thoughts, I could easily take the low road that leads to desire. Internal conflict is a constant fight between flesh and spirit. It's our desire opposing our wisdom with both fighting for control.

Without a set plan, we tend to negotiate a bit too much with the stomach, and when that happens, we all know who wins! But if I accept those chocolates with the foreknowledge that a small treat after dinner is in line with my plan, I don't have to negotiate. I can rely on a plan rather than impulse. Two chocolates come out of the box, and the rest are put into the cupboard and out of sight until the next day. The plan doesn't mean you necessarily have to start counting calories; it could mean envisioning the size and frequency of your meals beforehand, then sticking to the rule. This is where wisdom takes over and willpower takes a backseat.

The same thing can apply to exercise. The familiar line, "I plan to exercise more often from now on!" What does that mean? "More often" can mean once, or it can mean daily. If you leave the choice up to whim, chances are you'll opt for the minimum rather than the maximum workout experience. Be precise. Develop a regime you will stick to. For example, if your plan is to walk for forty minutes five times a week, map it out by deciding ahead of time when you'll schedule your walks, where you'll be walking (treadmill, outside, etc.). And if you can find a partner, then jot down whom you'll be with. By scheduling a time, we move it into our life and begin to shift things around it, rather than trying to squeeze it in where it fits. Priorities have a way of squeezing out the less pleasant activities, unless we make a point to prioritize them.

In a 2008 interview with Larry King, actress Ricki Lake, famous for losing over a hundred pounds and successfully keeping it off for over a decade (way to go Ricki!) said, "It's all in moderation; I think it's being consistent; I think it's being conscious of what you put in your body. There's no magic pill, there's no secret—it's hard work and being consistent." She added, "Any diet works, I've done them all. If you stick to it, they all work. But you have to stick to that plan."

The "plan" makes us conscious and aware of what we're putting into our bodies and how we are taking care of them, by fine tuning our focus. It eliminates bad habits while establishing good ones. When we prioritize items within the plan, we aren't wasting energy or spinning our wheels.

Evaluation is also important. If you aren't getting anywhere with your weight-loss plan, take a close look to see where you need some adjustment. Remember that if you're drinking calories in addition to your meals, cutting them out will benefit you. Consider portion size to see if you need to cut back. Look at the extras like gravy, cream, and dressing to see if they are an issue.

Setting a goal to lose slowly is not something most of us want to do, but it's a good way to go, and the truth is that time does go by fast. Imagine being fifty-two pounds lighter next year at this time. That's only one pound a week. Likely one frustrating, hair-pulling pound at a time, which calls for plenty of patience, but imagine the difference it would make! That is if you even had fifty-two pounds to lose. Maybe it's that last ten, twenty, or remaining baby weight of thirty pounds. Develop a plan, roll up your sleeves, and get the job done.

In formulating a plan that works best for your life, I'd like to offer you this snippet of wisdom:

If you want something you've never had before,
you have to do something you've never done before.
—Author unknown

Think about that. Doing mediocre work won't get you in fantastic shape. If you want to wear a different pair of pants, you have to live differently. Living differently doesn't mean you need to change the world around you, but it does mean you will have to make changes within. That's doable!

Watch thin eaters for a while, and you'll soon discover that most of them have a natural tendency to eat just enough. They haven't made eating a form of late-night entertainment, and eating isn't on their mind 24-7. In other words, it isn't their god. That natural tendency to eat just enough and to look at food as fuel rather than entertainment can be a part of you, too, over time. I don't look at food the way I used to anymore. I don't count calories, and I don't have to concentrate on stopping when I'm full. I've become so accustomed to living this way over time that it's ingrained in me now.

The plan I started with in the beginning was one that would fit into my lifestyle: eat the food that I love in moderation and exercise on a regular basis. I counted the cost, decided that I wanted to look good and feel great, and then did the necessary work to get there. I lost twenty pounds when I was seventeen years old and after each pregnancy was able to return to that comfortable weight once again. I've even dropped another five pounds in recent years staying at the lowest and the leanest weight I've ever been in my adult life. My clothing fits well, I have more energy than I did at sixteen, and I have learned the value of working and the return that it brings.

The Pantry
CHOCKED-FULL OF FOOD FOR THOUGHT

The Main Ingredient

Mapping out a plan, considering both the pros and cons beforehand, and deciding how to handle those cons will bring you that much closer to reaching success. There are so many plans out there that fit a wide range of lifestyles. Therefore it only stands to reason that some will be a good fit while others won't work well for you.

You may need to try a few out before you find your particular niche. The idea is to find one that not only works to bring you results but is also a lifestyle plan you would be willing to commit to for life.

A Slice of Advice

Dear Candace,

I grew up watching you on television. I am now thirty-three years old, and I recently became a mother to a beautiful little girl. She proved to me that God doesn't let you know how wonderful and amazing motherhood is until you have a child. My daughter is the single greatest joy in our lives, and we cherish her every day.

Anyway, on to my question . . .

I have been on your Web site and viewed your beautiful pictures and can't help but think, How does she look so good, and stay in such great shape after having three kids? I was quite thin prebaby, but I haven't managed to get my body back in the eight months since she was born.

Any advice on how you got into shape after your babies? I am breastfeeding (I'm not sure if you did as well), therefore I can't go on any strict diets, but I'd love to hear what your diet and exercise regimen were like postbaby.
—Marnie

Dear Marnie,
Congratulations on your daughter! Eight months and breast-feeding, huh? Surely you can shed a few pounds. My sister is breast-feeding and her son is four months. She called me this morning to tell me she dropped another pound.

No, you can't go on any strict diets, but you can certainly eat healthier and exercise more. Walks with the baby in the stroller are perfect. Start doing it five days a week! I also loved doing exercise DVDs when the kids were taking naps (or before they woke up).

Eat fresh foods—meaning no processed foods with ingredients listing words you can't pronounce! If it grows in the ground or on a tree and God made it without man fixing it up, eat it! Eat lots of fresh veggies, fruits, and lean proteins like chicken, turkey, and fish. I keep my portions small and try not to stuff myself. Halfway through, I check myself, "Am I satisfied—not full, but satisfied?" If so, I keep the rest for later.

It all comes down to your intake of calories. It's no big secret. I don't have any miracles. I eat healthy and I exercise. You can do it too! If you're not sure how to "eat healthy," there are lots of good books or programs that can help you learn like the South Beach Diet or Weight Watchers. Because you're breast-feeding, you can keep up your calories, but make sure they're good calories and not from high trans fat foods and soda pop.

Here is my plan in a nutshell:

- *Stop eating when you're satisfied.*
- *Don't eat fried food or traditional fast food.*
- *Watch your daily intake (from cheeses and cream based foods)*

- *Don't drink soda pop or sugar drinks.*
- *Eats lots of fresh veggies, fruit, and lean proteins.*
- *Keep desserts to a few bites.*
- *Snack on nuts (seven to ten).*
- *Drink lots of water.*
- *Get some exercise!*

—Candace

A Pinch of Practicality

If you want to take off the weight, or you're looking to create a healthier lifestyle, then sit down for a while today and map out the plan. Remember that weight loss is all about calories in and calories out. Better health requires that you give your body the required nutrients it needs.

Start by using the Internet to find out what each plan has to offer and how that would fit into your life. There will be some pain for some gain, but remember, this plan is for life.

The United States Department of Agriculture provides food guidelines for the average person as well as new moms and moms to be. You can find that information online through a quick search. It's a great place to start if you're looking to formulate your own plan. And guess what, moms? It also offers guidelines for your child's plan too.

Also consider your activity, and weigh it against your life. If you're not that energetic, then you may choose to implement a rigorous workout plan for yourself. You'll find several "calories burned" calculators online that can help you make an informed decision.

Finally you can consider the simple plan I live by, which I've outlined above in the "Slice of Advice." Maybe that one will work best for you too.

Make notes on each plan, pray about it, and then make your choice.

Food for Thought

A recap of Scripture to meditate on:

- Suppose one of you wants to build a tower. Will he not first sit down and estimate the cost to see if he has enough money to complete it? For if he lays the foundation and is not able to finish it, everyone who sees it will ridicule him saying, "This fellow began to build and was not able to finish." (Luke 14:28–30)

- Therefore do not worry about tomorrow, for tomorrow will worry about itself. Each day has enough trouble of its own. (Matt. 6:34)

The Candy Dish

The reason most people never reach their goals is that they don't define them, learn about them, or even seriously consider them as believable or achievable. Winners can tell you where they are going, what they plan to do along the way, and who will be sharing the adventure with them. —Denis Waitley

Grain Mustard Pork Chops

Serves 4

INGREDIENTS

½ cup grain Dijon mustard

2 teaspoons herb garden seasoning

1 teaspoon crushed garlic

1 teaspoon honey

2 tablespoons freshly chopped parsley leaves

1

pounds thick-cut boneless pork loin chop

DIRECTIONS

In a small bowl combine the mustard, herb garden seasoning, garlic, honey, and chopped parsley. Reserve ¼ cup of the rub for serving.

Transfer mustard mixture to a resealable plastic bag. Add the pork chops and thoroughly coat with the mustard mixture. Let the pork chops sit for at least 5 minutes or as long as overnight, in the refrigerator, before grilling.

Heat a grill pan over medium heat. Grill the chops for 6 to 7 minutes per side.

Transfer to a serving platter and serve sprinkled with the reserved rub.

FIVE

Heads Up, Eyes Forward, Shoulders Back

While other celebrities were running on treadmills—heads up, eyes forward, shoulders back—I held on to a broomstick (sans broom), feet planted firmly on my living room floor. I was sixteen and about to experience my first significant weight loss.

My mom had a talent agency representing both children and adults, and since a client of hers was a personal trainer, they offered me his services. My weight was never an issue from the producers on *Full House*, but knowing how sensitive a teenager can be about her appearance, my parents wanted to provide me with the knowledge and opportunity to get healthy.

While it wasn't a secret that I didn't feel great about my body, it wasn't a major issue either. The idea of getting myself in shape, living healthier, and losing a few extra pounds sounded good, so we invited him over to give it a try.

Starting at 5:30 a.m., four days a week, forty-five minutes per day, we worked out consistently in the living room of our house, using only a broom handle and two five-pound dumbbells, letting my body do the rest of the work. That, combined with both discipline and willpower, created results.

We also talked about my eating habits. One of the things he advised, which has stuck with me for so long, is this, "Eat until you're satisfied. Not full—satisfied."

As I previously mentioned, most restaurants serve you at least double the portion size you should actually eat. So I suggest stopping halfway through your meal to ask yourself the following questions:

- Am I satisfied right now?
- Am I satisfied if I don't have another bite?
- Am I still hungry, or is it just in my head?

These are the questions we need to ask until we're trained to recognize the hunger and full signals God has naturally provided to teach us to stop. Most people eat far past the full signal moving on to seconds and thirds and then on to dessert.

If you're concerned about wasting the food, then take it home. If you get hungry an hour later, great, then have a few bites of that meal in the fridge. Or if you are at home, put it away and pull it out later. Learn that you don't need to eat food just because it's sitting in front of you. If you're worried about passing up a dessert that is too good to resist, order one for yourself and take it home to eat later. Even if you're at a dinner party, most hostesses will graciously pack a dessert for the road if you explain that you're full. And remember, you don't have to eat the whole thing, just a few bites to satisfy that sweet tooth.

Even when it's just a sandwich, a muffin, or a power snack, train yourself to ask, "Am I satisfied?"

That's what I started doing. And what I realized, along with having stopped halfway through my meal, was that my stomach was shrinking, and I no longer required as much food. I realized how much I had been eating in the past, compared to how much my body actually needed. It's a simple concept, but one of the best pieces of advice I received.

I remember one of the first times I met Pete. We were sitting in my parents' living room, and I was drinking a fruit-flavored iced tea. He looked at me and said, "I see what you're drinking, and you probably don't think it's bad because it's got some real fruit juice in it, but let's take a look at the back."

He turned to the label and showed me the amount of calories and sugar in it. And he said, "You know, you could be eating some delicious food for the amount of calories that you are taking in just from this drink."

Up to that moment, I had never really thought about the fact that the calories I consumed in beverages were wasting valuable stomach room that I could be saving for the food I really loved.

He went over things like basic foods to avoid like anything fried, creamy sauces and dressings, high fat cheese and dairy and taught me to cut back on sugary drinks. He didn't eliminate these foods completely but suggested that I limit them and start making alternative, healthier choices.

Pete was great, calling me almost every day, at the end of the night asking, "Okay, what did you eat today?" Or he would call randomly just to check up on my progress asking, "Hey, how'd you do today? How are your workouts coming along?" I wasn't going to lie to him because I knew that ultimately the scale would tell him the truth at the end of each week. I was honest. His constant support and encouragement were a great motivator that got me off to a great start.

I worked with Pete for about a year and a half. After formulating good habits, I went on to work out at some gyms and do stuff on my own, which fit in with my work schedule. Let's face it, having a personal trainer wasn't cheap; it does get expensive, but he gave me an incredible foundation that jump-started my journey to living healthy on my own.

No, not everyone has the opportunity to have a personal trainer. I realize that. But it doesn't mean you can't have the benefits of one. The buddy system offers many of the same benefits—having someone beside you, checking in, offering motivation, and being that encourager. But here's the thing: I have a couple of friends that when we get together, we motivate each other to eat poorly. We become girls who say, "Hey, we're together. I love junk food, and you love junk food. Let's go get sundaes and pig out!"

And so sometimes those kinds of friends can be detrimental to your goal. They certainly aren't bad people, but I think we need to choose wisely when it comes to who we buddy up with. It's so important to have a buddy plan, but I know that we all have some friends out there that we tend to eat worse with when they are around, whether we both want to lose weight or not. My point is to choose wisely. *Will this friend stick with it, or will she cave quickly if you do?*

When it comes to your body, be a leader. Never fall into the role of a follower because it may lead you to stumble when you least expect to.

If you know you are a natural-born leader, find someone who has significantly less self control because it puts you in that position where you know you have to be the strong one, or vice versa. If you know you are weak and that you will cave the minute someone else does, then it's important that you find someone who already works out or is in good shape. You might ask, "Hey, can we team up and work out together?"

In addition to trainers and buddies, we have an additional support system on which I have relied, Jesus Christ. When the changes we make are anchored in the will of God and when our love for God becomes the driving force in our lives, we discover the ultimate trainer is with us, cheering us on.

Newton's famous law of inertia states that an object at rest will stay at rest and an object in motion will stay in motion unless an outside force is brought to bear upon it. For this reason, when we make our minds up to lose weight, outside forces can be an asset or a liability to us.

You know how it is: you set out vowing never to eat chocolate again, and you do well for two weeks until a little girl is standing at your door with a box of cookies in hand, offering you a slice of heaven for only five bucks. You reach for your wallet, all the while convincing yourself that it's for the sake of the kids. The cookies sit on the counter for a few days while you decide who you'll give it to. After two days you take one piece, and then two. Okay, so you decide you'll introduce chocolate back into your diet but only a wee bit after dinner. A wee bit turns into a bit, and before long a bit turns into a bit too much. That's when you find yourself right back where you started, and once again you are a ball in motion until something stops your momentum.

For me that something is a mind renewed.

And be not conformed to this world: but be ye transformed by the renewing of your mind, that ye may prove what is that good, and acceptable, and perfect, will of God. (Rom. 12:2 KJV)

We all have goals. Some of mine include being a good wife and mother, building my acting career and production company, having a well-managed home, keeping my body in shape, losing and now maintaining my weight. These are some of the things I strive for.

The good thing is that they've all been possible to achieve with God leading the way.

The force that brings me out of the state of inertia is the lane switch I take when I stop following my own way of thinking and start following His. That's the constant renewing of my mind also known as "walking after the Spirit."

It's been difficult at times to pass on scripts I've been offered when I know that other actresses would jump at the chance—to trust beyond a doubt that His plan is better than mine. But that's when I put the car into park, slide over to the passenger seat, and let God take the wheel. How do I know that His way will be better than mine? Because I trust that since He was faithful to me in the past, He will be the same faithful God in my future. If you believe that the direction you're taking is in accordance with God's will for your life—and I believe that healthy living is—I encourage you to press on in faith!

Reverend Richard Cecil once said, "We are urgent about the body; He is about the soul. We call for present comforts; He considers our everlasting rest. And therefore when He sends not the very things we ask, He hears us by sending greater than we can ask or think."

Understanding that God is able to do exceedingly abundantly above all we ask or think keeps us pressing toward our goals. When we finally change the way we think and start walking in the light, we are able to achieve our goals. This hope for the future is power for the present, and it's power that will move in your life.

Matthew 4 tells us that after Jesus fasted forty days and forty nights, He was tempted by the devil. What harm could it have caused if He had yielded to temptation and eaten one slice of bread? There are times when I also consider, "What harm, if any, could this one guest appearance be? It's a popular show that would definitely boost my career. Yeah, it doesn't reflect good moral judgment, but . . ."

And then I remember Jesus chose not to sin but to trust. He rebuked the temptation, saying, "Man does not live on bread alone, but on every word that comes from the mouth of God" (Matt. 4:4). His ability to press on proved that He rested on the strength of the Father and on Him alone.

I witnessed God's faithfulness and attention to detail in my own life with the unfolding of "Summer," the character I currently play in ABC Family's *Make It or Break It*. When the execs and I discussed creating her at our initial meeting, I never asked that she be made a Christian. That was something I only discovered after, when the producers decided it would be a great element to add to the show. It's been awesome to share many of the same values and faith as the character I play and to go to a job that I love every day. Now if I could only be as organized as Summer, I'd have it made!

Jesus understands the struggles I face with being a Christian in Hollywood, balancing family, friends, career, and the struggles I've had with food. That's what makes Him the ultimate trainer in my life. His mercy and grace add strength to my life. He not only equips me with the wisdom I need, but He is also the constant companion who motivates and encourages me every step of the way.

You might be reading my testimony but find yourself skeptical since every past attempt to lose weight has ended in failure. I hear you, but this time I'm suggesting that instead of relying on your strength alone, you draw strength in three ways. Why three? Well, first the Bible tell us that "a chord of three strands is not quickly broken" (Eccl. 4:12), so that's one reason, but I'm also suggesting this because "every matter must be established by the testimony of two or three witnesses" (2 Cor. 13:1).

Who are the three witnesses? God, yourself, and a partner:

1. Stay in communion with God.
2. Monitor your behavior.
3. Buddy up, and be accountable to a partner.

This matter of two or three witnesses has not only been echoed throughout the Bible; it's one I echo so often in my own life too. When I have a problem, a decision, or excitement to share, I often run to God, to Val, and to my best friend Dilini, whom I can trust for wisdom, encouragement, and support. Something about the number three completes the circle for me.

So while other celebrities are running on treadmills—heads up, eyes forward, shoulders back—I hold on to my God, feet planted firmly on faith. I'm thirty-four and still walking this journey of faith.

The Pantry

CHOCKED-FULL OF FOOD FOR THOUGHT

The Main Ingredient

A friend with a similar mind-set offers many of the same benefits a personal trainer can. Having someone who's encouraging you, is willing to check in to keep you on track, and can offer practical tips that are working for her is a blessing. It's especially great to have a walking buddy or a partner to take to the gym. But in addition to that, we have God, who's available 24-7. God, yourself, and a friend—combine the three and you have one unstoppable force!

A Slice of Advice

Dear Candace,

I've been following you your whole career. I loved you on Full House and still do. I've seen all your TV movies on Lifetime and Hallmark. My kids and I watched you on That's So Raven and now we're watching Make It or Break It.

You seem to look better and better as you age! You've certainly slimmed down over the years, so can you tell me what you do? I'd really like to know what you eat on a daily basis. Thanks!
—Molly

Dear Molly,

Thanks so much for being a lifetime fan! I hope I'll continue to make good movies and TV shows you'll want to watch for many more years.

I certainly have slimmed down over the years. I really refined my diet about eight years ago and have stuck to it ever since. Because our bodies change as we get older, I've realized that I had to adjust and streamline my diet with each passing year. Even the amount of food I could eat three years ago is slightly different from today. It's true that as we get older, we have to work harder. I've kept a close eye on the foods I eat and the exercise I do, and I know what works well for my body. My body and I have a strong relationship, working together to stay fit, strong, lean, and healthy.

Here's an example of what I may eat in a day:

Breakfast:
1/2 cup of cottage cheese on 1 slice of wheat toast with lots of black pepper on top
1 grande decaf, nonfat latte

Lunch:

Salad bar: Dark green lettuce (I pass up the iceberg because there is not as much nutritional value in it, nor does it keep you full for very long), tomatoes, garbanzo beans, cucumber, onion, broccoli, cauliflower, beets, raisins, with a scoop of tuna fish or pulled chicken. I also stick to a clear dressing like olive oil and balsamic, Italian or shiitake mushroom. I measure out two capfuls of dressing and pour over my salad, or keep it on the side and dip my fork into the dressing before each bite. You'll realize just how little dressing you need when you do it this way. And it saves a whole lot of calories!

Snack around 4 p.m.:

1 cup of fresh berries or a banana. If I'm really hungry, I may roll up 2 turkey slices with a piece of low fat mozzarella cheese, lettuce, and some spicy mustard.

Dinner:

Palm-sized piece of lean meat (chicken, pork tenderloin, or fish), four pieces of asparagus, and a side salad. I keep away from breads at night. Two pieces of dark chocolate for dessert (2 times per week).
—Candace

A Pinch of Practicality

There is a popular acronym known in the land of the lean as HALT. It means that when you feel like reaching for food, ask yourself first if you are hungry, angry, lonely, or tired. If you're hungry, then proceed, but if you are reaching for food in response to emotion, then halt your behavior immediately and deal with the problem at hand.

There's nothing inherently wrong with putting food to your mouth, but if you're doing it to fill a void that should be handled another way, then you're not being the best manager that your body deserves.

Next time you're mindlessly looking for something to eat, ask yourself if any of the following are eating at you:

- Hungry
- Angry
- Lonely
- Tired
- Depressed
- Guilty
- PMS
- Thirsty
- Stressed
- Discouraged
- Wounded

Any one of these things can knock you off your game should they remain unchecked. Some of them are easy enough to correct, while others may require some soul searching, prayer, and counseling.

Food For Thought

A recap of Scripture to meditate on:

- And be not conformed to this world: but be ye transformed by the renewing of your mind, that ye may prove what is that good, and acceptable, and perfect, will of God. (Rom. 12:2 KJV)
- A chord of three strands is not quickly broken. (Eccl. 4:12)
- Every matter must be established by the testimony of two or three witnesses. (2 Cor. 13:1)

The Candy Dish

Two are better than one, because they have a good return for their work: If one falls down, his friend can help him up. But pity the man who falls and has no one to help him up! (Eccl. 4:9–10)

From My Stove to Yours

Bacon Brussels Sprouts

Serves 6 to 8

INGREDIENTS

12 ounces thickly sliced lean bacon (or turkey bacon), cut crosswise
  into thin strips
1 Spanish onion, thinly sliced
8 garlic cloves, halved lengthwise
2 pounds Brussels sprouts, trimmed and halved
Coarse salt and freshly ground black pepper

DIRECTIONS

In a large, deep skillet, cook the bacon over moderately high heat until browned, about 8 minutes. Using a slotted spoon, transfer the bacon to paper towels to drain. Pat off excess fat. Add the onion and garlic to the pan, reduce the heat to moderate and cook, stirring, until softened, 3 to 4 minutes. Remove the softened vegetables from the pan and set aside. Add the Brussels sprouts in batches and continue to cook, stirring occasionally, until they are golden brown on the outside. Add the reserved bacon and vegetables to the Brussels sprouts in the pan along with salt and pepper to taste. Cover skillet with a lid and cook, stirring occasionally, until sprouts are just tender, 10 to 12 minutes.

SIX

Dressed in Designer Genes

Looking back at the wardrobe I had on *Full House* it's hard to believe that many fans considered me a fashion icon back in the day. Yellow scrunched socks, printed oversized sweaters, MC Hammer pants, Doc Martins, and big bangs set the look for DJ Tanner, television's young fashionista. And let's not forget the shoulder pads. From about the age of eleven, I had shoulder pads under nearly every outfit I wore. In fact the wardrobe department had a special pair made for me that snapped onto my bra straps so I could wear them full-time. Why, I'll never know. I could certainly understand wearing them under a blazer, but pajamas and T-shirts with shoulder pads just didn't make sense.

I've accepted the return of 1980s fashion even going as far as to embrace a pair of leggings of my own, but I still can't bring myself to wear shoulder pads or let a scrunchy enter my house. Can't do it.

It's interesting to note that people on the Internet are still asking how to style their hair like DJ Tanner. And others, noticing that it went from curly to straight, ask if I curled it every day. Here's the story on the hair: it's naturally straight with a little wave. During the summer before the second season of *Full House*, I got a perm, so I came to the set with it already curly. Once the perm grew out, I wore my hair straight with bangs that had a lot of volume. Not the standard straight-up 1980s style but a sort of winged shape that covered my forehead. I originally had it styled that way at a swanky salon in Beverly Hills, and taking the style back to the hairdressers on set, we realized they couldn't quite get the same look. So the producers and my mom decided I'd go to the salon in Beverly Hills every tape day morning and have it done there before heading over to the *Full House* set.

When I consider Andrea Barber's wardrobe, I really can't complain. Kimmy Gibbler was the epitome of fashion at its worst, and on those rare occasions when the wardrobe department let us dig in and take some of the clothing home, Andrea got the wee end of the stick.

Even though I was admired by thousands of young girls around the world, I still struggled with my own imperfections, concerned about weight and concerned about boys. We women are funny that way.

Things are looking up these days as far as wardrobe goes. Summer, the character I play on *Make It or Break It*, has the cutest designer duds. While most of the girls on the show are wearing leotards, I'm dressing in Trina Turk and Rebecca Taylor outfits. On an episode titled "Are We Having Fun Yet?" I wore an outfit by Theory, which was a short purple satin skirt with a silvery silk tank top that had a few ruffles across the front. It was topped with a black sweater adorned with jewels around the neckline. Black tights and black booties, completed the fun party look. Summer definitely has a sense of style, and I'm loving it!

The fun thing about being fitted while you're on a TV show is that there is a seamstress on hand, so everything is tailored and fit perfectly for me. It's so disappointing to go shopping after and find that things don't fit off the rack the way you know they can.

When I'm at home with Val and the kids or just hanging out with my friends, I'm most comfortable wearing jeans. I love my True Religions, my Rich and Skinny, and my Citizens of Humanity. And since it's so warm in California, I throw on a tank top, slip on my Havaianas and I'm ready to go.

I love fashion. Shopping seems to be my specialty, and living in LA gives me the opportunity to visit so many great stores. Shopping on Main Street in Santa Monica and then stopping at an outdoor cafe for a spinach salad (dressing on the side) and cold drink makes for a great afternoon out.

People are always asking me about my style and how to stay current. The key to finding those pieces is to TRY, TRY, and TRY them on again! Most of us gravitate toward the styles we've always worn and feel comfortable in. Don't be afraid to step out of the box once in a while. Only you and the dressing room mirror will see if it's really that horrible. I do think it's important to go shopping with a trusted friend whose opinion is honest and hopefully has some sort of fashion sense. If I could go with each and every one of you, I would! That's how much I love shopping. I'm even known to do my own version of *What Not to Wear* with my friends and their closets. Oh, I'm getting excited just thinking about it! I like to step out of my comfort zone and try things on that I wouldn't normally buy. As a result, I'm often surprised at how different something looks on my body than it does on the hanger.

I love shopping at department stores because of the enormous selection, but boutiques are great because of the personalized attention, helping me find the shapes and styles that fit me best. One more secret of mine—I'm a *Lucky* magazine subscriber. This practical fashion and shopping magazine gives me ideas on what's new, where to find it, and what fits my body type best.

As a Christian, modesty is also important. It's something I struggle with at times because everyone's view of modesty is different.

For some the idea of fashion is frustrating to say the least. Going to the mall isn't all that fun when you're restricted to oversized clothing at oversized prices. Wearing the fashion is frustrating when muffin tops are spilling over your jeans, underpants show every time you sit down, and skinny jeans are anything but skinny. I hear you, girlfriend.

Clothes, makeup, hair, weight, and wardrobe—let's keep it all in perspective. It's fun to look pretty and to feel good while doing it, but I often remind myself that this outer shell is simply an envelope for my spirit. The contents are precious, eternal, and costly, bought with a price, and the envelope has been fashioned by the world's greatest Designer, the Creator Himself. We are each God's one-of-a-kind design, and there isn't a single person in this world that's a match.

I encourage you to read and meditate on Psalm 139:13–16:

> *For You formed my inward parts;*
> *You covered me in my mother's womb.*
> *I will praise You, for I am fearfully and wonderfully made;*
> *Marvelous are Your works,*
> *And that my soul knows very well.*
>
> *My frame was not hidden from You,*
> *When I was made in secret,*
> *And skillfully wrought in the lowest parts of the earth.*

Your eyes saw my substance, being yet unformed.
And in Your book they all were written,
The days fashioned for me,
When as yet there were none of them. (NKJV)

Perhaps you're a size sixteen, you're basically happy with yourself, but you longed to be a few sizes smaller. You might even feel that shedding a few pounds would give you more energy, add to your health, and give your figure a more feminine appearance. You may even dream of the day when you finally walk into a mall and find that the styles you like fit you well.

On the other hand you may ask yourself, *Is it really God's will, or is it my own? Does God care if I'm a size sixteen or a six? Does God care if I lose weight?*

Let me first say this: God loves you, just the shape you are, and there isn't a single number on the scale that could ever change that. Do you know how enthralled He is with your beauty? How He knows the number of hairs on your head, and how He treasures every minute you spend quiet in His presence?

Yes, He loves you just as you are, regardless of your size, and there is nothing average about you or His love.

But let me also say that God designed the female body in a beautiful form—curvaceous, soft, and feminine. He understands the desire we have to walk across the mall, to slip into smaller sized pants, to like the reflection we see, and to hold a form of beauty both inside and out. After all, He created all things beautiful, from the smallest detail of a flower to the vastness of the midnight sky.

And while He loves us, He has given us the opportunity to improve our quality of life, but ultimately you will have to make that choice. No one will make it for you. Only you can weigh the cost and make that decision.

Is it God's desire that I care for my body? Since it's the temple of the Holy Spirit, I have to say yes. Many health concerns are out of our hands, but in many cases a healthy body is a reflection of an inner life that is balanced and one that has exercised self-control.

> *But the fruit of the Spirit is love, joy, peace, patience, kindness, goodness, faithfulness, gentleness and self-control. Against such things there is no law. (Gal. 5:22–23)*

If your body is rolling you out of bed instead of you rolling it, you've gotta wonder what your heart is thinking.

We can start by living by the Spirit while we stop following the heart of discontentment and doubt.

Countless potential dieters are sitting on the proverbial fence. They desperately want to jump over to the other side where new life begins, but fear and doubt spring from the heart, holding them back. Remember, the heart will deceive us with all sorts of negative thoughts:

- You're getting older, and older people can't take off the weight.
- You've tried so many times before, and you'll just fail again.
- Your family is overweight, so you will always be that way too.
- You're too far gone; it would take years to get back to a normal, acceptable size.
- Your husband likes you overweight, so why bother.
- You like food too much; it's not worth the effort.

Do any of the following thoughts affect your self-image?

- I'm not attractive.
- I'm fat.
- I'm a loser.
- I'm too masculine.

- I'm not accepted.
- I won't be good enough until . . .
- My body is disgusting.
- Nobody could ever love me.

I hope you don't contemplate any of these thoughts, but unfortunately many women who can't take off weight do.

The simple fact is that if these negative, destructive thoughts are growing in your heart, you will be as you think. If you let those thoughts remain in your heart and accept them to be true, they will eventually blossom and form who you are. If you wake up in the morning only to look in the mirror with disgust, you have already started out on the wrong foot.

If you want to live a life free from the bondage of food, the pull of the refrigerator, and the discomfort of those nasty waistbands, then start living that life today. You are beautiful, interesting, accepted, and loved by the most high God. Be content with both the woman you are today and the woman you'll be tomorrow.

You don't have to look back; just keep looking forward. Maybe you failed before—so what? Failure from the past is not a reason to give up today; in fact it's the very reason you should press on and make it work this time. Change what you can. You hold the God-given power to do that, and the great news is that He doesn't expect you to do it alone.

What is it about helium balloons that light up a room so elegantly? Or that make children squeal with delight? Are they not the same as the ones we blow up at the kitchen table and let drift to the floor? No, they aren't. Nothing says, "It's a party!" like a grand bouquet of pink and white helium balloons. What makes them different is that one floats and the other one sinks. It's that simple. What we put into them makes all the difference in the world.

We're hardly different. We are set apart from the crowd by the things we fill our minds with. "Whatever is true, whatever is noble, whatever is right, whatever is pure, whatever is lovely, whatever is admirable—if anything is excellent or praiseworthy—think about such things" (Phil. 4:8). These messages help us rise above our strongholds. These thoughts bring us closer to the person God created us to be.

What thoughts cloud your mind? Do you believe you can and will do what you set out to do, or do you entertain negative thoughts that whisper, "You can't"?

Believing in ourselves but, more importantly, believing in God as our source of strength will change us from the person we were. We shouldn't want to be anyone else, but we can be the best God created us to be. It's that familiar prayer of hope:

> *God grant me the serenity*
> *to accept the things I cannot change;*
> *courage to change the things I can;*
> *and wisdom to know the difference.*
> *—Reinhold Niebuhr*

The first step is to believe in yourself enough to get off the fence and step on to the other side. Hedging on the idea of losing weight but arguing with every thought that keeps you from it holds you in bondage and will continue to do so until you break free. Turn off the negative thoughts, and start believing in who you're created to be.

Growing up, the biggest boost to my confidence was having a few special people around me who always told me, "Candace, you can do it! You're talented and gifted. Go for it! It's okay if you don't make this one, keep trying."

Those words throughout my life helped mold me into the woman I am today, and if not for them, I don't know that I'd have the confidence to do the things I'm doing.

I was recently asked on the red carpet what body part I like best about myself and which one I hated the most. I delightfully answered, "I love my legs. They may be short, but they sure are shapely!" I thought for a second about which part I didn't like, and before I could let all the nitpicky things flood my mind, I didn't give it a chance. I reached for the Scripture stored in my heart and told her that God said I was fearfully and wonderfully made. And that I was going to stick with that thought.

God carefully thought of every detail in your wardrobe, providing you with a unique set of designer genes. Things that you think are imperfections are God's own craftsmanship. In fact the most beautiful things about us are usually those things we don't see in the mirror. It could be the way we tilt our head when we laugh, a glint in our eyes when we smile, or the way we carry ourselves into a room. Delight in yourself knowing that God made you just the way He wanted you to be. Own it.

The Pantry

CHOCKED-FULL OF FOOD FOR THOUGHT

The Main Ingredient

God created each one of us in our own unique way. Just like a snowflake we all hold a blueprint that differs one from another. It's great to lose weight and keep our bodies healthy and strong, but it's also important that we appreciate who we are today—with or without extra pounds.

Dear Candace,

I just want to tell you what a blessing you are, and how happy I was to learn that you are a committed Christian! I am thirty-eight-years-old and watched you back in the Full House *days. I have always loved you! Seeing you as the woman you turned out to be is such an inspiration. I have been a Christian since I was seven and was so blessed to grow up in a wonderful Christian home. It is so amazing to see someone like you with a heart like mine.*

You are so beautiful on the outside and, more importantly, so beautiful on the inside. One can truly see God's love in your countenance.

I have a couple of beauty questions: What kind of makeup do you use (base and powder)? I have the hardest time finding something that doesn't look like I have on a ton of make-up. Also, what kind of shampoo and conditioner do you use? Any deep conditioners or hair masks? I have hair similar to yours (color and length). It takes a lot to keep colored hair healthy, so any tips would be great.

Also, when you get your hair cut, how do you tell them you want it cut? I LOVE your hair!

Thanks, Candace, for reading my e-mail. Just know what a blessing you and your Web site are!

—Deb

Dear Deb,

Thanks so much for the sweet e-mail.

To answer your questions, I use a mineral-based powder foundation for everyday. It's light, easy, and quick to put on, just giving an even skin tone to my face. When I'm working on camera or hitting the red carpet, I use a heavier liquid makeup because of the lights. I use Frederik Fekkai hair products. I have fine hair but a lot of it. It's the most resilient hair my hairdresser has even seen. I'm blessed with that because my hair shouldn't be in as good of shape as it is since I've been coloring and highlighting it since I was twelve.

I trust my hairdressers and usually explain the type of cut I want. Layers are a must for long hair, or else it can be shapeless and lifeless in my opinion. A few months ago I decided to cut some bangs and am having fun with it. They do a great job with my hair, and I've never been unsatisfied. That of course is with my two trusted hairdressers: one in LA and one in Miami. It took a lot of searching, bad cuts, and color in between to find these people worth sticking with.

If you don't have a regular hairdresser that you love and trust, I'd take a picture of someone whose cut you'd like to emulate. That should help!

—Candace

A Pinch of Practicality

Weighing yourself once or twice a week is a great way to keep watch over your progress and slide backs. If you are up two or three pounds, you can ask yourself why and make changes before you start feeling too large in your clothes. By the time your clothing starts to feel snug, it's often a case where you've had five to ten pounds of excess weight creep up. And if you often wear stretch pants, you might not realize you are going off track at all.

If you have a comfort range, keep an eye on it. Make sure you stay in that target area, and if you see an increase of four or five pounds, then start cutting back before it goes any further. If you can catch it when you're four pounds up, instead of waiting until your buttons pop, you'll only have small changes to make. Catch it early. The numbers can matter when they are in a healthy range for your size.

Food for Thought

- For You formed my inward parts;
  You covered me in my mother's womb.
  I will praise You, for I am fearfully and wonderfully made;
  Marvelous are Your works,
  And that my soul knows very well.
  My frame was not hidden from You,
  When I was made in secret,
  And skillfully wrought in the lowest parts of the earth.
  Your eyes saw my substance, being yet unformed.
  And in Your book they all were written,
  The days fashioned for me,
  When as yet there were none of them. (Ps. 139:13–16 NKJV)
- But the fruit of the Spirit is love, joy, peace, patience, kindness, goodness, faithfulness, gentleness and self-control. Against such things there is no law. (Gal. 5:22–23)
- Whatever is true, whatever is noble, whatever is right, whatever is pure, whatever is lovely, whatever is admirable—if anything is excellent or praiseworthy—think about such things. (Phil. 4:8)

The Candy Dish

Trust yourself. Create the kind of self that you will be happy to live with all your life. Make the most of yourself by fanning the tiny, inner sparks of possibility into flames of achievement. —Golda Meir

Breakfast Sandwich

Serves 4—Your kids will love these!

INGREDIENTS

Nonstick cooking spray

4 eggs

4 whole-wheat English muffins

4½-inch round slices Canadian bacon

1 large beefsteak tomato, sliced into ½-inch slices

Salt and pepper

DIRECTIONS

Crack the eggs into a bowl and whisk. Add a dash of salt and pepper.

Put a quarter of the egg mixture into a skillet and cook, omelet style, until the eggs are cooked through (about 1 to 2 minutes per side). Do this four times (once for each egg).

Next, heat the Canadian bacon in a skillet until warm (about 1 to 2 minutes per side), and while that's cooking, lightly toast the English muffins.

Layer the English muffins with an omelet folded to fit, a piece of Canadian bacon, one slice of tomato, and the muffin top.

SEVEN

Unlock Your Freedom

Yahoo! was incorporated, "O. J. Simpson" was on everyone's lips, digital video discs otherwise known as DVDs were invented, and Boyz to Men were topping the charts. It was 1995. *Full House* was writing their last curtain call, and everywhere you looked, people were listening to Sheryl Crow.

While the end of the Tanner family closed one chapter in my life, God was busy writing the next. In the fifteen-plus years since the last curtain call, I have continued to move forward in my own life, realizing new dreams, overcoming surmountable struggles, and experiencing life to its fullest, all possible with four keys that God has so graciously placed in my hand. I stand humbly at His feet, thankful not only for revealing these keys to me but also because He is now using me as an instrument to hand them to you.

Each key is simple yet holds a unique strategy. When combined with the other three, they have the power to lock doors in our lives—such as addiction, depression, and doubt—and open new doors to our future that mark pivotal points in life's walking paths. These life-changing strategies have helped me. I have used them to grow my family and my character as a wife, speak to audiences of more than ten thousand people, launch my own T-shirt line, establish a presence on the Web, maintain a twenty-five-pound weight loss, publish this book, and land my current role in *Make It or Break It*. These four keys are actions we're all familiar with, but what many of us aren't familiar with is the freedom and sustaining power that the four provide when used together.

We've talked about the reasons our diets can fail. Now let's talk about the necessary keys to success!

Key 1: Willpower

Willpower is the one that most of us will hold in our hands several times throughout the course of our lives. It's the mind-set that moves us to say, "I really want to lose weight this year," or, "I want to buy a treadmill and start running each night," combined with the power to take the first step. Note that it's more than just good intention. Willpower is accompanied by self-controlling action.

It has the ability to control impulse. So if you are an impulsive eater, trying to stick to a plan without willpower, you'd be rowing a boat without paddles. Without willpower, there is nothing to harness your will—nothing to control your desires. It's an inner strength that keeps you going even when you doubt that you can. Using willpower to control your appetite and diminish bad habits is the first key to reshaping your life.

It does carry power, but willing and doing must go hand in hand if you expect to make progress. That's easy to understand, but choosing to live it isn't always as easy.

A good way to strengthen your willpower is through attitude. Self-deflating thoughts send messages to the brain that weaken your resolve. Decide to conquer those thoughts before they take root by thinking positively. Be determined in thought.

Take this for example. Anyone living in Santa Monica has heard of the stairs, and if you're any kind of athlete, you've probably run them a few times yourself. Joining 4th Street to Adelaide Drive, two long flights of stairs (totaling 174 steps) mark a landmark for athletes wanting a cardio and glute workout combined. I love walking them, but here's the thing: it's not just enough for me to say, "Val, let's walk the Santa Monica stairs in the morning." What I need to do instead is say, "Val, we should walk the Santa Monica stairs in the morning. I'm setting the alarm clock to get up at 5:00 a.m., which is actually great because we can watch the sunrise together."

Willpower means that I'll put that will into *action* by getting myself out of bed an hour earlier so we can get out there before our busy days get underway. This means that some mornings I'm crawling out of bed as early as 5:00 a.m., but at the end of the day, I can look back and see that each of the choices I've made have added up for the good.

Willpower holds the mind-set that obstacles are merely opportunities that can be climbed over to reach better heights. That's where "If there's a will, there's a way" comes from. If we decide to lose weight, we can let circumstance dictate our choices, or we can press on regardless of what stands in our way. Events like losing your job, having a spat with your husband, or the fact that you haven't slept in two weeks are all the kinds of stress inducers that offer reasons to support an excuse.

Preparing our minds to deal with these stressors before they take place by realizing that (1) some or several are going to take place and (2) when they do occur, I will look at them as an opportunity to thicken my skin, we are taking a sure and steady first step.

Willpower can move us to reach for our dreams, but willpower without the other three keys won't carry you through. So let's move on to the second one.

Key 2: Belief

We all have days when we wake up in the morning having lost faith in ourselves. Sometimes it's a result of eating far too much the day before. Sometimes we've said things we wish we could take back, but we can't. Other times we just feel like a failure because we see our tireless efforts as fruitless. All we can think of is how much of a failure we are; the future seems bleak. When it does seem bleak, we might convince ourselves to give up because the course ahead is too hard. That's when it's time to hop out of bed, put on your favorite T-shirt and jeans, do makeup and hair if you need to, then smile in the mirror and say this, "Failure does not define who I am." We all fail, we all make mistakes, and we've all done and said stupid things that we wish that we hadn't. If we let discouragement define our future, we are letting go of the reins we hold. When we stick with the program and believe in ourselves, we are able to grow from the experience and develop a stronger sense of who we are and what we are capable of.

> It's not who you are that holds you back, it's who you think you're not. —Author Unknown

If you don't believe that you can successfully lose weight and keep it off, then first, give your head a shake; second, look at the world around you just to see the countless people who have set out on a difficult journey and realized their dreams. I am living proof that belief in action produces results, so the next time someone tries to tell you that diets don't work or that nobody keeps the weight off, quote Henry Ford and reply, "Whether you think you can or think you can't, you are right."

Crash diets don't work, agreed. But it's a proven fact that good eating and exercise habits will produce good results. It's simple. But deeper than that lays the fact that belief has the power to move us where human strength cannot.

Marathon runners are often advised to use human strength for the first three quarters of the race and reserve the mental strength for the end. There's something about encouragement, belief, and conviction that drives us to reach places our flesh alone cannot.

In Matthew 17:20, Jesus says, "Because you have so little faith. I tell you the truth, if you have faith as small as a mustard seed, you can say to this mountain, 'Move from here to there' and it will move. Nothing will be impossible for you."

Belief in oneself can carry a man to the top of a mountain, whereas belief in God can move that mountain aside.

A perfect example I can share with you is that of my cowriter, Darlene Schacht. Darlene suffered severe dyslexia as a child and couldn't even read an entire book, let alone write one. When she first felt the calling to be a writer, she decided to glance into the mirror each morning and say, "Good morning, author."

It felt silly at first, but because she felt that God was moving her in this direction, she wasn't about to argue with Him. She approached me to write this book about four years ago, and although we faced several obstacles along the way, we kept pressing on, believing it would happen. We both knew in our hearts that this was His plan unfolding. It would have been so easy for us to give up the first year, but because we persisted, we can look back and see the direction the book has turned, and know that God has been unfolding this plan in His time.

Not only have we published this book, but Darlene is published in several others as well. That's the power of faith moving mountains!

There have been nights when we've been awake at 2:00 a.m. to pray about the book or prompted to grab a pen and literally take dictation as God breathed words into our hearts—sometimes several times a night. In the end we realize that we are nothing without Him other than instruments holding a pen, waiting for divine direction. How can we not believe when we see how God animates our bodies? He desires that we have life and that we live to our full potential.

Believing in ourselves doesn't mean that we replace God in the process. It means we believe He created us for His glory and pleasure. I'm sure He doesn't want us to wake up on the wrong side of the bed, discouraged over the mistakes we've made. He has given us life, and we can either live that life with joy, believing that we can make a difference, or we can wallow in sorrow believing we can't.

God wants us to have an abundant life. Does that mean we won't have struggles, poverty, or sickness? No. We will still face obstacles while in this human shell, but we will face them knowing that the sun always rises, and we are equipped with the ability to move past them each day.

Key 3: Decision

The accumulation of small decisions carries us farther than one decision ever will. Each year, each week, each day, and each hour we are offered choices. Should I grab water or a soda pop, a bag of chips or an apple? Should I drive or walk, take the stairs or the elevator? The reason we fail to consider these choices as carefully as we should is because the value we place on them is so low. We look at them as individual events that pale in comparison to the big picture we hope to create, but what we don't see is that with any masterpiece every brushstroke counts. Even the glint in one's eye can add life to a painting.

Initial decisions as well as constant decisions need to be on par. I know of a ten-year-old boy, one of Val's hockey fans, who dreamed of one day attending a Calgary Flames game. Only earning five dollars per week allowance the first year, and ten dollars for each week in the next, he saved every single penny for two years. While other kids purchased snacks from the canteen at school, he happily declined each and every time, believing that his final goal far outweighed the smaller pleasures in life. This year he hopped on a plane with his dad, stayed in a nice hotel, and realized the dream of his life. He was also excited to find out that I sent him some autographed hockey cards from Val's days with the Flames.

How many times have you reached for junk food that wasn't part of your plan because you justified that it would be a one-time thing? "Just this time" is a mind trap, and although we've fallen into that trap several times, we keep telling ourselves the same lie. Recognize the thought, and fight it. If a ten-year-old boy can figure it out, can't we?

> *Submit yourselves, then, to God. Resist the devil, and he will*
> *flee from you. (James 4:7)*

When we resist temptation, it eventually leaves. I promise you that. I mean seriously, you aren't still craving that chocolate bar you rejected last month are you? The temptation eventually left. Maybe it took minutes, or it might have taken a few days, but it does leave us alone. And on that note I'll also tell you that the more we resist temptation the less often it creeps up to tempt us. I love sugar and I always have, but I don't struggle with it the way I used to.

Once I started limiting and controlling my intake, my body became less accustomed to asking for it. That stands to reason. If a child is used to getting ice cream every day, he'll ask for it often, but if a child only gets it once a year, ice cream won't be on his mind.

Concentrate on the small decisions as well as the large, and before you know it, your masterpiece will unfold.

Key 4: Action

If we don't control our actions, they will control us. Recently I've been all the more keen on listening to God's Spirit and *acting* as the Spirit moves me. We hear people say that knowledge is power, but unless we put that knowledge into action, it's useless.

I know that in order to accomplish all that I have to do, I need to set my alarm most days to wake me at 5:15. If 5:15 a.m. comes along, and I hit the snoozer three times, then I'm not taking the necessary action I need. My day will start off on the wrong foot, and things just won't get done.

I believe that God speaks to me—to all of us—ready to lead and inspire in every area of life. We just need to listen to His voice, then act. Whether it's about feeding the hungry in Africa or deciding whether I should take on a movie role, I feel the prompt of His leading.

It's never enough to say, "I want to do this . . ." or, "I want to do that . . ." if we aren't willing to take the necessary action to get the job done. Starting my own T-shirt line began with a thought that grew into a vision that is still growing today. With each step of that vision, I've had to roll up my sleeves, get to work, and put things in place. Watching the creative process unfold is fun, but it involves organization, time, and thought, which I must be willing to give, and I am.

My weight-loss journey has been no different. Continual action in motion has been a key factor in maintaining the weight. I don't always feel like working out. In fact I'm not an exercise fanatic like some people are, but I do it because I know that willpower, belief, and decision cannot stand alone.

Action means I'll have an active role in my life. I won't sit around waiting for things to change but will take the necessary steps to make it happen. Things that are important deserve nothing less than vigorous pursuit.

Four Keys Combined

The beauty of the four keys combined reminds me of the daffodil garden in Running Springs, California. In 1958 (Alma) Gene and Dale Bauer started planting a garden of daffodils, planting them one by one by one throughout the years. Today the daffodil garden is said to be the largest daffodil garden in the world. One look at the magnificent hillside immediately draws me in.

This mountain hillside, which was once a wilderness of poor rocky soil, is now drenched with daffodils. A breathtaking experience to the tourists it draws.

The countless daffodils reflect care, as stewards of God's creation, they labored in the land they'd been given. Man and woman side-by-side. But the unmistakable miracle we see—made by the hands of only two—is that perseverance yields fruit to those who are trained by it.

Gene Bauer planted the first forty-eight bulbs in 1958, describing her persistence by saying, "One at a time, by one woman. Two hands, two feet, and a body minus a brain."

The garden illustrates the God-given potential each one of us holds when willpower, belief, decision, and action combine. As with many things, the task of losing weight can feel overwhelming if you view the whole instead of each part. Each step of the way, like the planting of one daffodil bulb, is easy enough for one person to manage. Take only one, and then take another . . . until you arrive at your place of freedom.

One pound at a time, one prayer at a time, one day at a time. That's how I reshape it all!

A journey of a thousand miles begins with a single step.
—Lao-tzu, Chinese philosopher

The Pantry
CHOCKED-FULL OF FOOD FOR THOUGHT

The Main Ingredient

Many women live their entire lives in bondage to food, never discovering the keys to unlocking the chains. God has equipped us with every key we need to unlock our freedom and live a victorious life. If willpower, belief, decision, or action has let you down in the past, try combining the four for success.

At times it can feel like we're climbing a mountain, especially for those who have a hundred pounds or more to take off. But it can be done. You can be released from this bondage to food. With each step and each prayer, you are making a difference, so grab onto the keys and begin unlocking that freedom today.

A Slice of Advice

Candace,

I understand that you lost weight and have kept it off for years. I saw you in US Weekly magazine, and thought that you looked way younger than your actual age. It's amazing what health and fitness can do to shape up our bodies. Wow!

I am a Christian too. And when I found out that you and your brother Kirk were Christians, I was so excited that I went straight to your Web sites. I'm amazed that you're a mom of three and that you can still manage to look so good.

I have tried so many good diet plans, but I can never seem to stick to them for more than a few weeks. I did stick to one for about two years, and at that time I felt better than I ever have. Then slowly but surely I started slipping back into my old habits again. It's so frustrating because I know how I want to look and feel, but I can never seem to stay there.

Do you have any advice for me that could get me back on track, and then stay there permanently? I'd love to be able to say I lost twenty pounds ten years ago and haven't looked back, but I haven't been able to say that yet.

—Jenny

Dear Jenny,

I believe that good eating habits along with portion control and regular exercise can make a long-lasting difference in your life. You didn't mention the plans you've tried, but that's okay, because I don't think it's about the plan as much as it is the steps we take to putting that plan into action.

You can have a hundred people attend the same weight-loss meeting, and out of those hundred, half might succeed. You have to ask then what the other fifty were missing.

I believe we need four ingredients to move us along.

The first one is willpower. It seems like you have it to some extent, but I think that if you really had it, you wouldn't have to ask how to get back on track. Instead you'd be trying your hardest to stay there.

Next believe in yourself as much as you believe in me. I can't get you on track, but I'll tell you one encouraging thing, and that is that you can. Right this minute you have the ability to get right back on the wagon and stay there.

You need to stay in the right frame of mind, which tells you that getting off the plan is never an option. Decide to pursue it, and stay there. That doesn't mean that you can never have pizza or cookies again. It just means that you will be conscious and careful of what goes into your mouth.

If you don't know what steps to take, then I suggest starting with portion control. Eat until you are satisfied, and stop when you're full.

Finally, you have the ability to carry you long past a decade, but your actions will dictate if you do or you don't. Control your actions, and show them who's boss. After months or years of repetition, there is a place of freedom where we no longer have to try, because we naturally do.

Have fun, and let me know how it goes in ten years!
—Candace

A Pinch of Practicality

If you don't see yourself making the necessary progress you should, then I suggest you try the following exercise.

Take a piece of paper and divide it into four sections. At the top of each section, mark down the following:

- Willpower
- Belief
- Decision
- Action

Next I want you to fill in the section as your day moves along. Under the willpower section, list the things you want to do. Maybe it's control your appetite today, or get three loads of laundry done. It may be that you want to take a five-mile bike ride. Mark down several things you want to accomplish.

Under the "Belief" section I want you to list pats on the back. If you cleaned the bathroom, mark it down. If you stopped eating lunch when you were full, there's another. If you made a donation to your favorite charity, add that. By the end of the day, you will see that you have the potential to accomplish much. Also take time to list some "I cans" such as, "I can do all things through Christ who strengthens me." Or, "I can stop eating when I'm satisfied, and I will be fine when I do."

Decision. This goes one step farther than willpower. You will write down the things you want to do and the things you definitely will do. Make no mistakes about it, this column is not an option. You must carefully decide what is to be done and ensure that it gets done in the time frame you list.

The action column records the steps you have taken to ensure that willpower and decision are moving along. Mark down each step you take. This exercise will show your progress.

Set aside time to review it each night and to start a new list each morning until you feel that things are moving along on their own.

Food for Thought

The following list is a recap of the Scriptures we covered in this chapter. You may find it helpful to post them around the house on little notes where you'll see them often. The Bible is great encouragement for every step of the way:

- Jesus says, "Because you have so little faith. I tell you the truth, if you have faith as small as a mustard seed, you can say to this mountain, 'Move from here to there' and it will move. Nothing will be impossible for you." (Matt. 17:20)
- "Submit yourselves, then, to God. Resist the devil, and he will flee from you." (James 4:7)

The Candy Dish

Those who profess to favor freedom and yet depreciate agitation are people who want crops without ploughing the ground; they want rain without thunder and lightning; they want the ocean without the roar of its many waters. The struggle may be a moral one, or it may be a physical one, or it may be both. But it must be a struggle. Power concedes nothing without a demand; it never has and it never will.
—Frederick Douglass

From My Stove to Yours

Orange Chicken Fajitas

Serves 4

INGREDIENTS

1 package chicken breast tenders
2 yellow bell peppers
2 orange bell peppers
1 large white onion
¼ cup orange juice
1 tablespoon olive oil

Salt and pepper to taste

10 to 12 tortillas

DIRECTIONS

Wash and cut the peppers and onion into thin strips. Wash chicken tenders and cut them into strips as well. Heat olive oil in a skillet and add chicken tenders, peppers, and onion. Cook all until chicken is cooked through. Vegetables should be tender. Add orange juice and let simmer for another 5 minutes. Salt and pepper to taste.

Serve on flour or multigrain tortillas.

Top with shredded lettuce, light sour cream, and Mexican cheese (optional).

EIGHT

Live an Adorable Life

He's a big kid for his age, has a lot of love inside of him, and he's funny. Maks has a whimsical way of making people fall in love with him because his personality is outgoing and fun. He'll talk your ear off, tell stories, and steal your heart with his big smile and twinkling blue eyes. He's not shy in the least and likes food the most. He could sweet-talk a dog off a meat truck and is never at a loss for words.

He's a leader, and his friends know it. He'll march by the beat of his own little drum, and if they don't follow, he's content to march alone. Like other kids, he enjoys video games and the computer, but nothing gets his heart beating like hockey does. Maks is so into hockey, that's all he wants to be, and he could play with a hockey stick and tennis ball all day long.

A short while back Maks and I went off to a shoe store together—just the two of us. Since there was a sale on UGGs, and I had wanted a pair of UGG slippers, we decided to shop. Getting into our SUV, I saw that he had a stick and tennis ball he wanted to bring along, and after one endearing look from the boy, I agreed.

While I surveyed the shelves, looking for the right pair of shoes, this guy walked into the store and smiled at Maks, who was stick handling the ball. Maks was intent on shooting, and I was intent on scoring a new pair of UGGs. Looking over at the man, I noticed his familiar face was one I had seen several times before. This uncaped crusader had graced the big screen more times than I could count, charming us with his generous smile and sparkling blue eyes.

One flash of that smile told me he was amused.

Minutes later Maks was helping me pick out shoes, telling me which styles and colors he liked best. It was one of those great moments between mother and son that bond you together like caramel and corn. A day I won't soon forget.

With hockey stick in hand, Maks hustled out of the store chirping, "Mom, I need you to be goalie!"

Dropping my bags, I was ready to block.

Just as Maks shot the tennis ball, the familiar man walked out of the store, then stopped and watched us for a moment while a smile spread over his face. Walking toward his car, he passed us, while Maks called out again, asking me to be goalie one last time.

The man stopped to take a phone call while I caught the ball with one hand. "Nice catch!" he said. "I think you're the most adorable mom I have ever seen in my life!" Then he hopped in his Batmobile and drove out of sight.

That's a great compliment, coming from someone I admire so much, especially when being a great mom is at the top of my daily to-do list! It's also a great compliment to see my children warm the hearts of those around them.

They're joyful and happy children, but I know that their good behavior is a result of constant direction and training from both Val and me. We're their primary teachers in life. The words we speak and the actions we take today are shaping their future tomorrow.

It would be so much easier to pretend I don't notice when Natasha gives me a "look" or when Lev complains during chores, but I believe that being a good mom means I'll be wise enough to implement discipline as well as have fun.

In the same way I have come to accept that my body requires the same balance. It's great to have fun and let loose, but it's equally important to be self-disciplined. In Scripture after Scripture the Bible stresses the importance of controlling our bodies, our tongues, and our thoughts. Yet most of us would rather ignore that than put a microscope to the topic and get down to work. Not me—in this chapter I'm pulling out my microscope and getting down to the nitty-gritty business of controlling our actions.

Ask anyone who has reached a high level of weight loss, and they will tell you that it was a direct result of self-discipline. It's never easy in the beginning, but with each hurdle you pass, you get stronger. Self-discipline grants us the ability to seize bad habits and put them away, even those habits we want to hang on to. It gets our feet on the track when we're too tired to run and closes our mouth when we're filling our face.

Consider a race. The preparation involves self-discipline on the runner's part if she hopes to come in first, or in the case of long distance—if she hopes to finish the race at all. Self-discipline is an exercise that reminds our body that the Spirit is the one who's in charge. We as believers follow the Spirit of truth, and we do our best to stick to that truth as we yield to God's plan for our life. The world sees it another way: the body's in charge, and if the heart longs to overindulge in food or narcotics, it does. Yielding to our flesh is the easy way out, but in the end it produces damaging circumstances of various kinds.

Just like any exercise, we are strengthened by the continuing practice of discipline. And when we cease to exercise, we become lethargic. *So why don't we practice self-discipline?* The reason is because we're conditioned to take the easy way out. But when we condition our bodies to difficult tasks, we grow into disciplined human beings.

We taught Natasha to clean her bedroom, starting with small tasks, and increasing responsibility over time. As she grew, those habits became ingrained in her, but they also branched out farther than the walls of her bedroom. She has been able to apply the same self-discipline to practicing tennis, cleaning the dishes, and doing her homework each day. My point being that if we become disciplined with the small things in life, we will grow to discipline ourselves even further.

Ever notice that the first three days of any change program are difficult? The reason is that we are flexing a muscle that's been at rest for too long. The first week at a gym has most women talking about aches and pains from muscles they'd long forgotten they had. But as they begin to move those muscles on a daily basis, they're strengthened to the point where it becomes painless activity and, in some cases, to the point where it's mindless activity. That's also where muscle memory comes in. Our brains get conditioned to memorize motor skills like tying our shoes or braiding our hair. In fact it's rare even to look at the shoes we tie; we just do it because that muscle of our mind has memorized the movement we take.

Through self-discipline we exercise another part of our mind that eventually makes a habit of things we do like choosing healthier food, eating less at each meal, taking the stairs, or waking up early. We take control of our body and train it to yield to the Spirit.

Creating good habits requires three things:

1. Focus
2. Repetition
3. Action

Anytime we can combine those three, we are working toward long-term success.

Webster's Dictionary describes *discipline* this way: "Training that corrects, molds, or perfects the mental faculties or moral character." The idea here is *training*. It's important that our bodies are trained by repetition so the muscle of self-discipline is allowed time to grow.

I'm certain that if Maks was uncontrolled in the shoe store, high sticking the shelves, and running amuck while I did my own thing, we both would have drawn a different response from the customers there. But Maks makes me look good because he's good himself.

Excessive weight gain, yielding to addictions, and sloppy habits are often signs that we lead undisciplined lives. Controlled eating, fasting, exercising, addiction control programs, and strong devotional habits are signs that the body is under subjection.

> *I discipline my body and make it my slave, so that, after*
> *I have preached to others, I myself will not be disqualified.*
> *(1 Cor. 9:27 NASB)*

Practicing self-denial is another way to add strength to self-discipline. Try to incorporate little reminders every once in a while that tell your body it's not in control. If a pool is cold, jump in. If French fries smell delicious, choose salad. And if a must-see TV show is on in five minutes, retreat to a corner with a good book in hand—unless that show is *Make It or Break It*, of course!

In preparation for the task God had for Him, Jesus fasted forty days. Moses and Elijah are also recorded as fasting for forty days in preparation for the work God set before them. Denying a hunger within us increases a hunger for spiritual food. However, it is important that when we fast we aren't doing it for the purpose of losing weight but rather for the purpose of gaining spiritual strength and communion with God. Fasts can be dangerous if they are too long or if your body isn't in good enough shape, so be cautious. It's great to discipline our body but not at the risk of our health.

It's not something that happens overnight. Just like exercise, it can take several months of training for our muscles to build. Once I trained my body to yield to the Spirit, the fruit of self-discipline naturally became evident in my life. I was then able to incorporate wise eating habits, and because of self-discipline I've stuck with the plan. In many areas of my life, I've reached the place where self-discipline is a natural choice that doesn't feel like self-discipline at all.

If I'm out with a friend, I prefer to stop in at a café than opt for fast food. And if I'm at a café, I'll order something like a mixed green salad with grilled salmon (dressing is always on the side), and a glass of unsweetened iced tea. Self-discipline has carried me a long way since the "quarter pounder with cheese" days, and I'm still growing strong.

If you were near a movie theater in the mid-1980s, you probably watched the original *Karate Kid*; it's a classic. After the death of his father, Daniel (played by then heart-throb, Ralph Macchio) and his mother pack up and leave for California in search of a new beginning. Shortly after settling in, Daniel has a run-in with a local thug who brings him down with a few smooth karate moves. Ouch! It was painful to see little Ralph getting pummeled by a thug and his gang, but the harassment continues time and again until adorable handyman, Mr. Miyagi, appears and single-handedly takes down the gang. This is where the audience puts down their popcorn and whispers "Righteous" in true 1980s fashion.

Daniel eagerly becomes a student of Mr. Miyagi hoping to learn karate and kick some butt of his own. But if you remember anything about the movie, you'll probably remember that the training had little to do with karate at all. Daniel was assigned laborious chores like painting a fence, sanding a floor, and waxing one car after another after another. Aside from learning how to wash a car, disgruntled Daniel finally learned that serious training involved balance and that his training had as much to do with his spirit as it did his body.

It's never easy to accept the discipline part of any task we take on. Ask any kid who wants to help with dinner. Everyone wants to stir the soup, but nobody wants the nasty job of putting the food away or washing the dishes. Cooking a meal, joining a gym, starting a new diet, taking a class, teaching a class, starting a family, writing a book, getting a pet, and the list goes on. Most of the things we set out to do have a price—hard work. The cost of hard work is worth the final reward if we don't give up before seeing the end. Bringing our bodies into subjection with self-discipline is never fruitless activity; it only serves to enrich our lives further.

> No discipline seems pleasant at the time, put painful. Later on, however, it produces a harvest of righteousness and peace for those who have been trained by it. (Heb. 12:11)

To get a biblical view of self-discipline, let's take a closer look at the self-disciplined side of the woman personified in Proverbs 31:

- Works with eager hands (v. 13)
- Brings food from afar (v. 14)
- Gets up while it's still dark (v. 15)
- Plants a vineyard (v. 16)
- Works vigorously (v. 17)
- Is clothed with strength and dignity (v. 25)
- Speaks with wisdom (v. 26)
- Doesn't sit idle (v. 27)

Do some of those characteristics speak to you? Have you refused to work out because it would mean getting up a little earlier? Do you grab something quick to eat because you don't want to take the time to get your food from afar? Do you waste too much idle time on the computer or television when you could be enriching your mind? Are you clothed with strength and dignity, or do you throw on a ball cap, slip on a ratty old T-shirt, and then head out of the door praying you won't be seen?

Self-disciplines when applied to our life not only bring self-respect; they also bring respect from others around us:

- Her husband has full confidence in her (v. 11).
- Her husband is respected at the city gate, where he takes his seat among the elders of the land (v. 23).
- Her children arise and call her blessed; her husband also, and he praises her (v. 28).
- Let her works bring her praises at the city gate (v. 31).
- Shoe shoppers randomly say she's an adorable mom. (I added this one!)

When self-discipline is called for, many of us step back immediately. Although we don't outright admit what we're thinking, what we'd like to say is, "Uh, no. I'm not going to sign on to anything that requires sacrifice on my part. I'd rather wait until an easier plan comes along." And so we wait for the next quick fix that promises weight loss at no cost—maybe it's an all-you-can-eat soup diet or licking the pounds away on an ice cream diet. We fail time and time again because a quick fix doesn't strengthen us for tomorrow; it satisfies and gratifies the body today.

Losing weight and staying in shape is simple. There isn't a rock that hasn't been turned, no magic pill that waits to be found. It's a battle that needs to be fought; the only question remains: "Are *you* willing to fight?" If you put it off for tomorrow, you're waiting too long. Self-discipline doesn't know when it's Monday; it calls us to step up today.

A life of sacrifice is an act of spiritual worship. I don't suppose the Proverbs 31 woman particularly liked getting up while it was still dark, lighting a fire while the others remained warm in their beds. And I don't think it will be easy for you in the beginning either. The first time you pass up a bag of chips, turn down some chocolate, or settle for water instead of a can of soda will be difficult, but I believe without any uncertainty that in time you will be happy with the changes you've made.

Worship speaks to my heart and moves me to obedience. It's amazing, to be able to worship God by giving up a part of myself. Being able to give up the hold I had on the world as an act of worship to God. It's not always easy, but it's how I serve as a living sacrifice—giving up my will for His.

All things die that we may have life, so that nearly every piece of food we put in our mouth is a sacrifice in some way or another. Beef, chicken, pork, fish, lettuce, carrots, and the list goes on—all living things that have died so that I might live. Nature itself typifies the death and resurrection of our Lord, bringing glory to God.

Dying to one's self is an act of worship. Each time our body yields to the spirit, we reflect the passion of Christ in our life—a passion that's worth fighting for.

> Then he said to them all: "If anyone would come after me, he must deny himself and take up his cross daily and follow me. For whoever wants to save his life will lose it, but whoever loses his life for me will save it. What good is it for a man to gain the whole world, and yet lose or forfeit his very self?" (Luke 9:23–25)

The Pantry
CHOCKED-FULL OF FOOD FOR THOUGHT

The Main Ingredient

We're talking about self-discipline. It moves us to challenge our bodies—reminds the body that it's not in control. When we challenge our bodies and win, we reap the benefits that come with self-discipline. Once we train our bodies to yield to the Spirit, the fruit of self-discipline will naturally be evident in our lives. We'll then be free to incorporate wise eating plans and to stick to those plans.

Self-discipline is an exercise that strengthens us over time when we continue to implement it. It puts our spirit in control of our flesh and keeps putting it there until the flesh learns to follow.

A Slice of Advice

Candace,

I think that you are in amazing shape, and although I thought you were a beautiful teenager, I think you're absolutely gorgeous now! Even your hair and your skin glow. Are you on any specific diet plan, and are there any foods that I should avoid if I want to lose weight and improve my glow?

—Bev

Dear Bev,

Rather than refraining from food, I have retrained my body to eat smaller portions. There aren't any foods that I see as taboo, but I do limit them far more than I used to. I look at it this way, "All food is permissible, but not all food is profitable."

However, when making healthy choices for yourself—especially if you're looking for that glow, limit foods cooked in butter. Use Extra Virgin Olive Oil instead. Cut back on fatty condiments like mayo and creamy dressings, and opt for nutrition-rich foods like fruit, vegetables, and whole-grain breads. Beware of pastas in rich sauce. I do enjoy them but only on occasion and in an appetizer portion. Watch your dairy, and switch from whole milk to skim. Eat red meats less often, but enjoy white meat and fish.

If you want your skin and hair to glow, drink water! I love water, and it's always my first and favorite choice.

Aside from diet, I'm very active, working out about five days a week. I jog, walk stairs, and can't live without Pilates!

I will also add that I believe the glow has a lot to do, if not all to do, with my faith.

I've been told by strangers, "There's something different about you. It's almost like you have a glow." I love the Lord with all of my heart, and I pray that it shows on my face.

I pray that with some good choices and a lot of self-discipline you'll find that glow too.

Thanks for your note, Bev.

—Candace

A Pinch of Practicality

Discipline comes in all shapes and sizes. In fact aside from the obvious with diet and health, we never know when a situation will call for self-discipline. It could be holding our temper in traffic or resisting a sample at the grocery store. But one thing we all have in common is a home, where we can start exercising self-discipline now.

Get into your closets, into your basement, and into your drawers—start cleaning them out. Get rid of things you don't need, even if you like them a bit. Let the new motto be, "If in doubt, throw it out." Get organized; get your house lean, and get your house clean.

Put your home on a diet and maintain the weight loss you attain. Because a home is a reflection of us, it's important that our surroundings reflect the same level of self-discipline we hope to achieve.

Here are a few ways to eliminate clutter:

- Go through your closets, and if you haven't worn an outfit in the past year, pack it away for the homeless.
- Rummage through your kids' toys, throw out the ones they don't use, and divide the remaining toys in half. Pack half away, and rotate them every couple of months.
- Go through your cupboards and discard any extra sets or odd pieces of dishes you don't normally use. After all, how many plastic bowls does one family need?
- Look around the room at your stuff. If it's not useful or pretty, get rid of it.
- Take a look in your linen closet. If your towels and sheets have multiplied over time, you can probably part with the old tattered ones.
- Look under the bathroom sink. What hair products, bubble baths, or scented soaps aren't you using? Give them away.
- Take a look at your cosmetics and discard extra lipsticks and eye shadows. If you aren't wearing them now, you probably won't.

- Thin out your garden. Give plants to your neighbors if they are growing too thick.
- Dare I suggest you part with some shoes? Come on . . . I know you can do it!

Living in a light environment gives us a sense of control and self-discipline that empowers us to start working inward.

Food for Thought

A recap of Scripture to meditate on:

- I discipline my body and make it my slave, so that, after I have preached to others, I myself will not be disqualified. (1 Cor. 9:27 NASB)
- No discipline seems pleasant at the time, put painful. Later on, however it produces a harvest of righteousness and peace for those who have been trained by it. (Heb. 12:11)
- Then he said to them all: "If anyone would come after me, he must deny himself and take up his cross daily and follow me. For whoever wants to save his life will lose it, but whoever loses his life for me will save it. What good is it for a man to gain the whole world, and yet lose or forfeit his very self?" (Luke 9:23–25)

The Candy Dish

Mental toughness is many things and rather difficult to explain. Its qualities are sacrifice and self-denial. Also, most importantly, it is combined with a perfectly disciplined will that refuses to give in. It's a state of mind—you could call it character in action. —Vince Lombardi

Oven Roasted Asparagus

Serves 4

INGREDIENTS

2 pounds of fresh asparagus
Olive oil
Salt
Pepper

DIRECTIONS

Preheat the oven to 400 degrees.

Wash the asparagus, and then cut off the tough ends. Peel if necessary. Place on a baking sheet. Coat the asparagus with olive oil, and then spread it out in a single layer on a baking sheet. Add salt and pepper. Roast until tender but crisp (about 25 minutes).

NINE

Don't Feed the Lions

In the wee hours of June 13, 1974, in Moscow, USSR, God was putting the final touches on his newest creation: a bundle of joy that would soon emerge on the ice as one of Russia's greatest hockey players and then the world's greatest husband. I couldn't begin to imagine my journey through life without the loving support of my husband Val.

Not only has he been the kind and supportive man I had hoped for; he's also a rock I can lean on when I need encouragement, a smile, or a shove out of bed for those early morning workouts we do. Whether we're off for a morning run on the beach or just kicking a ball with the kids, he coaches us on with games and challenges that work our bodies and minds while we're still having fun. One of our favorite workouts takes place at the beach. Val draws two lines in the sand about thirty feet apart, and while we're all feeling goofy with our hopping, squatting, and jumping, we're having a good time getting through an incredibly difficult workout.

While Val is training our children to be young athletes, he comes from a long line of athletes himself. His brother Pavel Bure, also a professional hockey player, has been named the Russian Rocket for his speed on the ice; and their father, Vladimir, was an Olympic swimmer (three-time medalist). Digging even farther back, we see that Grandpa Bure was a professional water polo player.

So how did I meet this amazing young athlete from Russia? Fellow *Full House* cast mate, Dave Coullier, pulled me over and introduced us at a charity hockey game. *Cute guy? Good hockey player? Thanks, Dave!* Since the Bure brothers had been watching *Full House* to learn English, he already knew DJ quite well. It was now just a matter of getting to know Candace, and I was all over that!

Like any marriage we've had our happy days and our growing pains (no pun intended), but it wasn't until nearly a decade into our marriage that I really began to understand the impact that my role as a wife could have in this union. With some changes of my own, I was excited to discover that an already good relationship could be transformed into a great one.

The first step I took was understanding that although marriage is an equal partnership where husband and wife are equally important, we aren't designed to share the same roles.

Holding the Bible, I read, "For the man is not of the woman: but the woman of the man. Neither was the man created for the woman: but the woman for the man" (1 Cor. 11:8–9 KJV).

Today's society had me believe that there should be no differences between a man and a woman. Society had it wrong. Val and I were created equally but differently, and so we have differing responsibilities in our marriage—mine being his helpmate. God created Adam, and when he saw that Adam was alone, he created Eve to be his helper.

Was this an important lesson in reshaping me? Very much so. Weight loss is as much about submission as it is about calories in and calories out. If we can learn to yield to the authority God has placed in our lives, in turn we learn that our flesh must yield to our Spirit. I can also put it this way: *your heart must yield to your head.*

We come from a world where submission is a thing of the past. If something feels good, we do it, regardless of conscience; children are disobedient to parents, and employees have little regard for employers. Yet the Bible teaches us time and again that God has put a chain of command in place for our good, even within our own self.

Our culture is full of talk about "following your heart." It's a common understanding of doing what *feels* right to us. This sense of "heart" is in the Bible, too. It refers to our heart as the "wellspring of life." For this reason we need to guard and protect it by guarding and protecting our desires. Remember when we talked about the "flesh" and that sense of innate desire? It will often tell us that we need something when we definitely don't. We don't need to empty a bag of chips before bed or down a stack of cookies with milk, but our flesh will often tell us that we do. It will also tell us to give up trying when the going gets tough. It's ruled by feelings.

Pop culture would have us believe that by "following our heart" we can never go wrong. This is why it's so important that we dig into Scripture and keep digging. Because when we do, we discover that it is our job as stewards of this human vessel to guide ourselves with wisdom according to truth.

Jeremiah 17:9 warns us, saying, "The heart is deceitful above all things and beyond cure. Who can understand it?" Obviously not those who, with flattering lips, say, "Follow your heart, dear."

Follow wisdom, and only wisdom, according to the truth laid out in Scripture. When I do, I find that it often contradicts with my heart until I get to the point that even my desires begin to surrender to wisdom.

The daily renewing of our minds by the Spirit of truth is important to gaining this wisdom. Teaching our minds to listen and yield to the Spirit lays out our inner road map directing the paths by which we should go; couple that with self-discipline that brings our body into submission, and we're on the right path.

Begin to disciple your mind first, by feeding it well. Once that is on track, you are equipped to start leading yourself:

Listen. Gain wisdom. Guide.

The way that we guide is by training ourselves to yield to a Spirit-focused mind, a mind that is daily renewed through Scripture, meditation, and prayer with our Lord. When I lead my body to spiritual food, the desires of the world fade away.

> "How sweet are your words to my taste,
> sweeter than honey to my mouth!
> I gain understanding from your precepts;
> therefore I hate every wrong path.
> Your word is a lamp to my feet and a light for my path."
> (Ps. 119:103–105)

I don't always feel like biting my tongue when an argument erupts. I don't particularly enjoy getting out of a warm bed to go work out. And I'd rather eat carrot cake after every meal than reserve it for occasional treats. But each of the small steps I take in yielding my heart to my head brings fruit of health and happiness to my life. It's not about instant gratification; it's about long-term success that offers a life of freedom from strongholds that have gripped us for years.

Today we live in a pleasure-driven world where gluttony is the norm, and thus obesity is on the rise. Back in the 1940s America didn't have the weight problem it has today. Following World War II, food was in short supply, and the little we had was rationed among the people. Our ancestors learned to survive on enough. They didn't eat until they were full, but they were given enough to survive. Not only did the war get the U.S. out of depression; it propelled the country into prosperity.

Prosperity gives us the option for gluttony, a sin the Bible warns against. But many of us aren't sure where pleasure ends and gluttony begins, so let's take a closer look at Scripture.

Proverbs speaks against a gluttonous lifestyle saying: "Do not join those who drink too much wine or gorge themselves on meat, for drunkards and gluttons become poor, and drowsiness clothes them in rags" (Prov. 23:20–21).

In the English language our word for *gluttony* is derived from the Latin word *gluttire*, meaning "to gulp down or swallow." The Old Testament often uses the Hebrew word, *saba*, which when used in a negative sense is defined as "to have in excess."

The modern definition of the word *gluttony* is "to habitually eat to excess." So what should we do about it? Proverbs 25:16 sums it up well by saying, "If you find honey, eat just enough."

When we look at Scripture, it doesn't sound a whole lot like God is telling us to "follow our heart." In fact, what we can derive from Scripture after Scripture is that it's our duty as believers to submit our desires and follow the Spirit.

An old native story describes how a young man was confused. Not knowing how to deal with his confusion, he approached an elder for some wisdom. Telling the elder that a lion and a bear constantly wrestled in his mind, the young man wondered which one would win.

The old man looked at him, put a hand on his shoulder, and wisely replied, "The one that you feed."

Which one do you feed? Do you feed your flesh by pampering it, giving in to every cry of the heart? Or do you feed your mind with the Word of God, which equips your spirit?

The reality is that when we submit our will to God's will and when we surrender our desires to delight ourselves in Him, He *will* give us the desires of our heart. Yet they will be desires that are in line with what is best for us because they have been guided by the wisdom of His Spirit.

The drive for some actors in Hollywood is status. The lure of riches and fame can be tempting. And for many it means giving up who they are in the process. For me, it's been different. I have given up who I am for the sake of Christ and Him alone.

Not to sound like a Hallmark card, but there is so much more to life than success and wealth, fame and riches. The draw for me is eternity. Life is short. Statistics show that ten out of ten will die. So the question becomes, Where do I want to spend eternity: heaven or hell?

Being a Christian who is trying to live a life that's pleasing to God doesn't mean life is a drag. I haven't lost out on anything; I've only gained perspective on life, peace, joy, fulfillment, and purpose.

God gives me all those things. That's something the world can never fulfill because it constantly begs me to get more, reach a higher status, and keep acquiring stuff. It never satisfies.

We are surrounded by advertisements that keep us focused on what we don't have, what we should have, and how we can get it. Everything to take our eyes off the fact that there is a Holy God to whom we'll be accountable.

The peace and joy in my life are not a result of my own perfect world. I still go through some of the same struggles I have in the past, and I experience new hardships. But the way I choose to deal with the anxiety has changed. When the old me got stressed, I turned to food for comfort. When trouble came my way, I'd mindlessly reach for that fix. But when I took it at face value, I realized that food wasn't a fix at all. It's a temporary high that masks the real fixing we need—peace with ourselves through the healing touch of the one true Comforter—the Holy Spirit.

We converse daily with the people around us, but the truth is that the majority of the conversations we have are internal dialogue with ourselves—thoughts. If we get discouraged, worried, annoyed, deflated, lonely, or sad, and we stay that way, it's only because we're feeding those thoughts and letting the lion win. In fact, we're probably agreeing with them if they're sticking around. If we tell ourselves that we're nothing all day, how can we ever look in the mirror and expect to see ourselves the way God sees us? If we tell ourselves that we won't succeed, how can we find the courage to be a success? We can't unless we start to change patterns in our thoughts.

Thinking is a choice we make minute by minute, day by day. In order to stay in the right frame of mind, so that we are equipped to overcome the enemy, we're instructed to train our thoughts. I train my body, and in the same way I've had to retrain my thoughts.

By thinking about things that are good, forming positive opinions of people, and keeping a good attitude when things start to look bleak, I keep my thoughts in check. Getting anxious or negative, and then letting thoughts like that fester, will lead to stress. Cast your cares on God the minute you feel them enter your mind. Look for the positive side of things when you can. And talk people up instead of cutting them down. When you are at your lowest, remember that you are always one thought away from happiness.

Peace is something that's hard to explain. It's a feeling that things will go well and that they in fact have already started to. Peace has the power to affect us both mentally and physically, lowering blood pressure and heart rate. It's a bandage for the heart and salve to the mind.

Our job starts by being alert. We need to interpret our thoughts wisely, divide the good from the bad, and with a little self-control (okay, maybe a lot) converse with our thoughts in a positive way. In other words, stop feeding the lions!

If life gives you lemons, you don't have to settle for lemonade. Did you know that one lemon could power a light? When attached to the right source, it can also power a motor. Imagine just for a moment what the lemons in your life could produce when God powers them! Poverty, sickness, addictions, and discouragement . . . the list is endless, but God's grace is not! Start turning those negative thoughts into powerful statements of faith by submitting your heart to your spirit today.

> *Cast all your anxiety on him because he cares for you. Be self-controlled and alert. Your enemy the devil prowls around like a roaring lion looking for someone to devour. Resist him, standing firm in the faith. (1 Pet. 5:7–9)*

Draw a line in the sand, submit your heart to your head, and have a good time getting through an incredibly difficult workout.

The Pantry

CHOCKED-FULL OF FOOD FOR THOUGHT

The Main Ingredient

We have learned that in order to be self-disciplined, our hearts must yield to our minds. But in order to equip our minds for the job, we need to keep that mind in the best shape we can. We do this by listening to the good and tuning out the bad messages in life. Focus provides us with the ability to improve our minds when that focus is fine tuned. Keeping our minds on track equips us to keep our bodies on track. That's what we need for success!

A Slice of Advice

Dear Candace,

I know that you often talk about self-discipline and how that relates to your life. I get that you turn down jobs if they don't line up with your faith, and you drag yourself out of bed when you don't necessarily feel like working out. Kudos to you!

I grew up watching you in front of the cameras, and I see that growing in God has made a difference in your life. You are such an inspiration to me.

My question to you is, how do you keep your mind on track? I get mine on track for a while, but then I keep slipping right back into old habits again.

—Donna

Dear Donna,

Thinking is a choice we make minute by minute, day by day. In order to stay in the right frame of mind, so that we are equipped to overcome temptation, we're instructed to train our thoughts. We train our bodies, don't we? So why not train our thoughts?

Start by being alert. Interpret your thoughts to divide the good from the bad. The Bible tells us to think about things that are noble, right, pure, lovely, praiseworthy, and admirable. If those thoughts are there, welcome them, nurture them, and allow them to grow; but if you have negative thoughts of any kind, try to recognize and eliminate them as soon as you can.

When we become anxious about things, we get stressed. Stress can tire us out, and it also gives us a reason to fall off the wagon. I eliminate stress by praying through it, working out, reading, or talking to Val. Find ways to eliminate stress and use what works for you before stress sets in.

Stay with it, Donna, repetition and perseverance is your friend!
—Candace

A Pinch of Practicality

Start to notice positive, inspiring, or empowering quotes around you and jot them down. You may hear them from people or read them in your favorite book. These quotes make great pick-me-ups when you place them around the house. Put one in your wallet that you'll see when you're paying for groceries. Put a few on the fridge that you'll read when you're busy cooking. Put one on the dashboard of your car to meditate on before you drive. Encouraging quotes can be packed with power to feed your mind and strengthen your resolve.

Thousands of quotes can be found online, or you can munch on a few from my "Candy Dish."

Set aside some time to pray, to read the Bible, and to listen to God speaking to you.

Food for Thought

A recap of Scripture to meditate on:

- For the man is not of the woman: but the woman of the man. Neither was the man created for the woman: but the woman for the man. (1 Cor. 11:8–9 KJV)
- The heart is deceitful above all things and beyond cure. Who can understand it? (Jer. 17:19)

- How sweet are your words to my taste,
  sweeter than honey to my mouth!
  I gain understanding from your precepts;
  therefore I hate every wrong path.
  Your word is a lamp to my feet
  and a light for my path. (Ps. 119:103–105)
- Do not join those who drink too much wine or gorge themselves on meat, for drunkards and gluttons become poor, and drowsiness clothes them in rags. (Prov. 23:20–21)
- If you find honey, eat just enough. (Prov. 25:16)
- Cast all your anxiety on him because he cares for you. Be self-controlled and alert. Your enemy the devil prowls around like a roaring lion looking for someone to devour. Resist him, standing firm in the faith. (1 Pet. 5:7–9)

The Candy Dish

"A pessimist sees the difficulty in every opportunity; an optimist sees the opportunity in every difficulty." —*Winston Churchill*

From My Stove to Yours

Candace's Famous Chopped Salad:

This salad is *so* easy to make, and it's incredibly healthy and delicious! There's no right way to do it. Just get chopping. If you're making it for yourself, chop about ½ cup of each thing. If you're making it for a group, go up to 2 or 3 cups of each ingredient!

INGREDIENTS

Broccoli

Cauliflower

Spinach leaves

Yellow bell pepper

Tomato

Corn (raw from the cob)

Avocado

Egg whites only (hard boiled)

Ham (deli sliced)

Turkey (deli sliced)

Salami (deli sliced)

DIRECTIONS

Chop everything into bite-sized pieces and mix! Add pepper to taste.
I drizzle a teaspoon of Extra Virgin Olive Oil after it is plated. I suggest doing so in case you have leftovers. This way it won't get soggy in the fridge.

Here's the key: The Avocado adds it's own oil, keeping everything together and flavorful. You really don't need any dressing because of it.

I only added pepper to taste because the ham and salami have enough salt on their own. Remember, salt in excess isn't good for you.

If you're a vegetarian, skip the meats!

Hard-boiled egg whites are pure protein!! If you need more protein in your diet, this is a great way to get it.

Aside from the meats and eggs, everything should be chopped raw. No cooking required! How easy is that?

Hope you enjoy this incredibly easy and uber tasty salad! It's lunch *or* dinner!

Mom took my first head-shot in our front yard at age four.

On set for one of my first commercials shot in New Orleans for Cascade Detergent.

One of my favorite commercial head-shots, wearing my mom's hat.

At age eight, I was recording a Chef-Boyardee jingle for the commercial. Notice my "audition" outfit: overalls, pigtails, and bows!

Brandy Gold, Emily Schulman, and I played ballerinas in a Kentucky Fried Chicken commercial.

At age ten, my debut on *Full House*. I'm standing in front of my dressing room door, rocking my Madonna look.

And then came the perm!

Full House went to Hawaii! Standing with Jodie, Mary-Kate, and Ashley on location. I was feeling great in my bathing suit!

Hanging out with Jodie Sweetin and Lori Loughlin on set.

Signing posters and autographing pictures
at a large venue to promote *Full House*.

In Hawaii with my mom,
one of my favorite pictures
of the two of us.

Standing with Scott Weinger on location
at Disney World for a *Full House* episode.
This was the heaviest weight I'd been in
my teen years and I wanted nothing more
than to hide in my hotel room.

My first official "date" with Val
in Fredericton, New Brunswick.
I was head over heels for him,
especially after he held me while
we skated together.

It was Dave Coulier who introduced us, but here we're with
Bob Saget at another charity
hockey game.

"Introducing Mr. & Mrs. Valeri Bure"—as
we entered our wedding reception!

Val is the love of my life. I thank God for him
every day and am blessed to be his wife.

My bridal party! Left to right: Dilini (my BFF), Shelene (check out
www.skip1.org), my super petite and oldest sister Bridgette, my cousin
Mackenzie, and my practically twin sister Melissa (with brown hair/eyes)
who is just eighteen months older than me.

Merging my *Full House* life with my new life. Left to right: Dave Coulier,
John Stamos, Lori Loughlin, me, Val, Bob Saget, Jodie Sweetin, Scott
Weinger, and Andrea Barber.

Three months pregnant with Natasha. I'm cheering on Val and team Russia in the 1998 Winter Olympic Games in Nagano, Japan. They took Silver.

Holding three week old Maksim in Salt Lake City, Utah, waiting for Val and team Russia to bring home another medal in the 2002 Winter Olympic Games.

Val brought home the bronze from Salt Lake City.

One of the happiest days for me in Val's hockey career, signing with the L.A. Kings! Unfortunately the excitement didn't last long when Val was sidelined for the entire season because of a hip and back injury during a pre-season game.

I love this picture of my kids! Natasha finally warmed up to getting another brother and Lev was thrilled to have one.

Getting some love from Natasha, Maks, and Lev at our house in Malibu, California.

This became our Christmas card picture taken in Aspen, Colorado. Snowball fight!!!

Lev loves the water—surfing, skim-boarding,
boogie-boarding, and body surfing—
all summer long in California.

Natasha models for one of my
favorite charities, Skip1.org.

Val showing Maks proper technique
while doing push-ups in the sand.
This goes along with our summer
beach workouts!

At the hockey rink
24-7, I'm thankful
Maks still needs my
help tying his skates.

Remember chapter 1? Here are the ducklings we rescued that soon went to the Wildlife Center.

At twelve years old, Natasha and I are practically the same size. She loves showing her strength by giving me a piggy back ride.

One of my favorite places in the world, Val and I love taking bike rides through Napa Valley.

Lev and Maks during a hard day's work. Lemonade anyone?

Inspired by *Make It or Break It*. Maybe there should be an episode where the gym moms compete?! At thirty-four, I feel like I can do anything.

Fourteen years and counting. I love my man, and love his passion for his second career . . . www. burefamilywines.com.

Val and I share the same anniversary date as mom and dad, June 22. My parents have been together forty years!

Our baby cocker spaniel, Emma. Don't let that sweet face fool you—she'll find your food and inhale it!

Sydney was power under control, always letting Emma win the battle over a sock.

Sydney, named after the character from Melrose Place, was a gentle giant.

Best Friends Forever—it's Kimmy and D.J.!!
Andrea Barber and I still keep in touch and see
each other at birthday parties and gatherings.

Here I am with my lovely *Make It or Break It* co-stars.
Left to right: Josie Loren, Cassie Scerbo,
Chelsea Hobbs, and Ayla Kell.

With the talented and
funny Tom Arnold
on *Moonlight and Mistletoe*.
I guess I should have let
him eat before I nabbed
him for a picture!

Meeting and greeting new friends and fans as
I sign CDs of my testimony while speaking at
Women's Conferences across the country.

On my first missionary
trip to Ghana, Africa,
with a loving team from
Getwell Road United
Methodist Church.

I'm blessed to be the
National Spokesperson for
National House of Hope,
a Christian residential program for troubled teenag-
ers across the country and
internationally.

Two of the biggest hams you'll ever meet:
Miss Mandy Young and me.

With my beautiful coauthor Darlene Schacht while on
the Music Boat Cruise to Mexico.

My travel bud-
dies: Alex, Lisa,
and Mandy Young.
That's a lot of
blonde hair!

Dilini and I have been best friends since the tenth grade.

My heroes: Mom and Dad

The Cameron Family, left to right: Candace, Melissa, Kirk, Robert, Bridgette, and Barbara taken in Malibu 2009.

Val inspires me to stay in shape. Gotta
love a professional athlete!

My precious family today. We're all about goofing around,
keeping it real, and keeping it fun!

TEN

Hey There, Delilah

The book of Judges tells us the story of Samson, a man of incomparable strength. He tore a lion apart with his bare hands, caught three hundred foxes, slew a thousand men with the jawbone of an ass, tore the gates from the city wall, pulled down the pillars that held up a vast house, thereby killing three thousand people, and had a weakness for women.

Chapter 14 tells us that his first wife deceived him, enticing him with tears for seven days, until he finally gave in. And again in chapter 16, we read about yet another woman, Delilah, who for the love of money sought out to discover the source of his strength. "It came to pass when she pressed him daily with her words, and urged him, so that his soul was vexed unto death; that he told her all his heart" (Judg. 16:16–17 KJV).

The story of Samson, whose secret to strength was his uncut hair, may well typify the power we have when God is on our head; but it also illustrates the power that persistence holds to weaken our strength. Even the strongest resolve becomes weak when faced with negative thoughts time and again.

Remember the saying, "The squeaky wheel gets the grease"? It means the ones who complain get all the attention. Luke 18 tells us that after a certain widow repeatedly approached the judge for justice against her adversary, he finally threw down the gavel and said, "Because this widow keeps bothering me, I will see that she gets justice." It's amazing what harassment can do.

I dealt with my fair share of repeated harassment in junior high. Seventh and eighth grades are difficult for most students, but for a girl on a TV show trying her best to fit into public school, it was even more so. I remember kneeling down at my locker looking for a math book I needed when suddenly my hair was yanked back and I fell to the floor. Another day I arrived at my PE locker to find it covered in shaving cream, gum, and the worst of written obscenities. Some kids would purposely bump into me as they walked down the hall and call me all kinds of names in hopes I would cry.

"Can't handle the heat, DJ?" they'd mock day after day as they ridiculed me. I understood their behavior was a reflection of jealousy, but that knowledge couldn't erase the insecurity that was building. Word by word they were wearing me down, until I finally I gave in to my tears.

Persistence has a way of wearing us down when day after day we're faced with the same set of circumstances. My parents explained their motives to me in hopes that would help, but it hurt just the same because they didn't let up.

Junior high was a struggle, but it served to remind me that the outside world can potentially affect the decisions I make. Bullies come in all shapes and sizes, their most common weapons being actions and words. If left unchecked, these weapons find a way of permeating our skin and piercing our heart.

As a mom who has learned from the past, I am equipped with knowledge to help my children by offering the following advice:

1. Avoid trouble when you know it's lurking around.
2. Pretend that you're brave even if you're not.
3. Find a buddy who will stand by your side.

Instead of conquering bullies, we need to focus on conquering thoughts since harassment travels through our brain before settling in. We can't change the world, but we can change the way we react to it. Neither words nor people can affect us without our thought pattern allowing them. Temptation acts much the same way. It's a smell, a sound, or a visual cue that travels through our thoughts before it becomes a desire.

Now let's consider the question, What's tempting you? Take one look in your refrigerator or pantry, and you might find the answer. Is it a pie? A chocolate bar? A bag of chips? French bread? Soda pop? Every time you walk into the kitchen and open the door, you see it. Sure you'll say "no." And the next time you walk into the kitchen, you'll say "no" again. And the next time, and the next . . . until you finally break down, pick up the pie and cut a thick slice.

James 1:14 tells us, "Every man is tempted, when he is drawn away of his own lust, and enticed" (KJV). I could imagine that verse referring to a drunk sitting in a bar lusting for the next drink. His clothing is torn and well worn; his beard is unshaven. His hand trembles while he holds it down with the other. He looks nothing like me, but one look in the mirror tells me I'm wrong. Temptation lurks at our doorstep no matter how polished it is.

Webster's Dictionary defines *enticed* this way: "To attract artfully or adroitly or by arousing hope or desire. Tempt."

It's no wonder we food lovers struggle to keep our hands off the munchies. The constant lure we present ourselves with wears us down. If we set out to make change in hopes of achieving success, we must also redesign our surroundings to ensure it.

Willpower gets us off to a great start, but temptations like "Betcha can't eat just one!" can eventually wear us down. "Out of sight, out of mind" is a proven fact when it comes to eating. The less temptation we face, the less we'll give in to it, so just as we handle our bullies—keep the junk out of sight and out of reach. Some people go as far as freezing their charge cards inside a block of ice so they are less likely to use them. Without the ease of availability, we don't give spending a second thought. By the time we thaw the block of ice, temptation has fled, and we can then ask, "Do I really need this or not?"

The same rings true for those things that are good for us. If you wash fruit and put it out where your family will see it, they're more likely to grab a piece here and there. You may even want to nudge the bowl in their direction every so often. Store some washed lettuce in the fridge, and you'll be more likely to make a salad. Place cold water in the fridge, and you're apt to drink some. Keep veggies washed and cut, and you'll likely grab a few. And let's not forget—keep the Bible close by, and you'll be reminded to read it. This is where availability becomes an asset.

Putting your healthy choices out front is a great way to design your life for success. It is the power of suggestion. We're faced with suggestions every day in one way or another—through commercials, billboards, aromas, magazine covers, the behavior of friends, and the like. If those stimulants are negative and we face them often enough, we're setting ourselves up for a fall. We can improve our chances by presenting our senses with good choices, and we are bound to succeed.

Design your life by avoiding the visual lure. Take weight-loss books for example. They are a pool of information, but weight-loss magazines are a pool of temptation. Try picking one up for encouragement and inspiration, and you'll find page after page contains glossy photos of food. Sure they have low-cal recipes to go with them, but rather than taking our focus off the food, the magazine usually brings our attention back to it. That would be fine if we didn't have an issue with food, but I suspect that most women who pick them up do. We could choose a recipe, head to the store, buy the necessary ingredients, and whip up a nutritious, low-cal meal for our family. That would be using it wisely. But unfortunately many of us have a problem that we're literally working our butt off trying to overcome, which is the lust of the flesh—the desire to overindulge, and the tendency that we have to glorify food more than we should.

A little piece of Scripture known as "the eye covenant" is found in Job 31:1, "I have made a covenant with my eyes; why then should I look upon a young woman?" (NKJV). Using Job as a role model, many committed husbands, like mine, have decided to make the same covenant with their eyes. If a beautiful woman walks by, a man may take notice, but if he gazes at her for a while, his mind will travel to places it shouldn't. So rather than looking her way, he turns his eyes and his attention to something else.

If this covenant helped Job overcome lust of the flesh, it can also work for you. This covenant would usher in a few changes for you, such as avoiding the snack aisles you used to browse, passing by free samples without stopping to consider what they're serving today, and replying, "No, thank you," the next time someone passes a cookie or a caramel your way.

If you spend the morning fantasizing over your lunch and the afternoon meditating on how great your dinner will be, then something desperately needs to change.

Of course there are times when it's appropriate to savor the goodness of food and consider what our next meal will be. But reserve those moments for when the time is right, which is when you're ready to prepare a meal or sit down to eat. Everything in moderation, that's how you'll manage to enjoy the journey.

An interesting book on the market combines two topics—psychology and food—*Mindless Eating: Why We Eat More Than We Think* by Brian Wansink. Brian makes a point in his book that rings a familiar bell. He writes about variety, saying that when we have a variety of food, such as an all-you-can-eat buffet, we tend to eat more. That's true when you consider the fact that "I'll have one of these, and I'll try one of those, and I'll taste a little of that" adds up fast. That's when it's important to eye your food first to decide how much to eat and don't put too much on your plate.

The next step in facing our bullies is to act strong even when we're not. It's a good step to take when overcoming the temptation to binge. Resisting temptation is the first step to seeing it flee. I don't always feel strong when I say no to a second piece of carrot cake. I might say, "No thank you, I'm good." When the truth is that I'm not good at all. I desperately want to have more, but I choose my action, and soon my body agrees with my choice. Like I said before, no matter what you crave, the feeling eventually leaves. Wait for it.

Sit up straight, push your plate away, and smile when you feel that you've had enough. If you grumble and complain about wanting some more, you're giving in to the lure of the food. Same goes for your workout. If you go into your workout with a mediocre attitude, you won't perform at top speed. Attitude fuels energy, so grab a good one and use it.

Last but not least, find a friend you can count on. Thankfully I had good friends growing up so I was never alone, but the best friends I could ever have were my sisters, Melissa and Bridgette. Melissa was just a couple of grades higher than me and was always prepared to gather her friends and come to my rescue. I didn't mind that! They've always been protective of me, which came in handy when I was stuck to a locker with gum in my hair and shaving cream on my face.

Having a buddy who understands our struggles and wants only the best for us is an asset when the going gets tough. If I'm ever feeling down and need a word of encouragement, I know that I can still call my sisters to give me the love.

Samson is a story of consequences. He left himself open for attack. All of the power he had available to him was lost because he wasn't attentive to the circumstances around him. He let the bully move in, take what was rightfully his, and leave him powerless in the process.

Bullies come in every shape and size, whether it's in the form of a person or a temptation we face. Avoid them at all costs, be brave when you're not, and find a good buddy who will stand by your side. That's how we stay strong; that's how "DJ" handles the heat.

The Pantry
CHOCKED-FULL OF FOOD FOR THOUGHT

The Main Ingredient

When steps are taken to establish a life-changing routine, sabotaging thoughts seem to find their way in. We can conquer negative thoughts by taking steps to avoid a run-in with them. Out of sight, out of mind is one of the best ways to control what we see. When we control what we see, we limit the lure.

A Slice of Advice

Dear Candace,

I really enjoy reading your advice. What a wonderful resource. Thank you for being the God-centered, Christ-loving woman that you are!

I, too, am a mother of three young children. Between Bible study, homeschooling, and caring for my home and husband, I struggle to find time to exercise and eat properly. I wonder, what is your secret to being so slim and healthy?
—Madison

Dear Madison,

My secret to staying slim and healthy is (drum roll please!) . . . eating well and staying active.

Okay, I know that was a pretty simple answer, but it's the truth. Over years of being on a weight roller coaster, I finally got to the point where I wanted to stay fit and feel good all the time. I always feel healthier and prettier when my weight is lower, and of course my clothes fit better. I had to change my eating habits and lifestyle once and for all. Luckily, my husband was 100 percent on board and was probably the biggest encourager to our family in this area. So eating habits changed not only for me but also for my children and my husband.

For me the key has been eating fresh, healthy foods and not overeating. I'd prefer to eat more of the yummy foods I enjoy in smaller quantities rather than eating large portions of only healthy foods that I don't really enjoy. For me eating is about the taste and not the quantity. A lot of women I know are just the opposite, and quantity is important rather than quality. You have to figure out what is important to you and get into a new way of eating from there.

Include your whole family. If you just try to diet on your own, it's not going to last for long. If you change your whole family's eating habits and fitness/sports routine, you'll have a better chance at sticking to it.

I take Pilates about three times a week as well as play tennis, and I walk about 1 1/2 miles every day (around my neighborhood). The kids either walk with me or ride their bikes. This turns into family time not only to share and laugh but also to exercise. (When the kids whine about walking the circle, telling them "no dessert" usually quiets them pretty fast.) And FYI . . . dessert is usually fresh fruit. They have ice cream or something sugary sweet once or twice a week. (And we keep that to a small portion.) Trust me, this makes the once-a-month trip to Cold Stones, for whatever they want, all the better!
—Candace

A Pinch of Practicality

Put away or throw away food that isn't in line with your plan. If treats are part of your plan, but you intend to have them in moderation, then put them someplace that is difficult to get to like on top of a cupboard or in the basement. You'll find that when you have to make an effort to get the food, you won't be as likely to repeatedly indulge.

Take a trip to the grocery store and pick up some healthier options like fresh vegetables, fruit, and bottled water. Take time to wash the produce and chop the vegetables when you get home to ensure that they are easily accessible.

Keep a fruit basket on the counter and a selection of cut veggies in the fridge.

Save your water bottles and refill them. Keep bottled water in the fridge at all times so you can grab one on the go. Also make a habit of grabbing a bottle each time you leave the house so you won't be tempted to stop for a sweetened coffee on the road. Piggybacking one new habit with a regular routine is a great way to introduce a new change.

Food for Thought

A recap of Scripture to meditate on:

- And it came to pass when she pressed him daily with her words, and urged him, so that his soul was vexed unto death; that he told her all his heart. (Judg. 16:16–17 KJV)
- Every man is tempted, when he is drawn away of his own lust, and enticed. (James 1:14 KJV)
- I have made a covenant with my eyes; why then should I look upon a young woman? (Job 31:1 NKJV)

The Candy Dish

When a resolute young fellow steps up to the great bully, the world, and takes him boldly by the beard, he is often surprised to find it comes off in his hand, and that it was only tied on to scare away the timid adventurers. —Ralph Waldo Emerson

Grilled Vegetables

I simply love grilled vegetables. They're wonderful hot off the grill or used the next morning in an omelet.

INGREDIENTS

Zuccini cut in ¼-inch thick lengthwise slices
Yellow squash cut in ¼-inch thick lengthwise slices
Eggplant, skin removed, cut in ¼-inch thick lengthwise slices
Scallions (long green onions)
Purple onion: cut into ¼-inch thick slices

DIRECTIONS

Place cut veggies except eggplant on a platter and drizzle olive oil generously over them. Sprinkle salt and pepper.

Using a basting brush, lightly coat eggplant in olive oil. Note: the eggplant will soak up the olive oil quickly. Don't worry if you can't see it. Sprinkle with salt and pepper.

Grill on low-medium heat until lightly brown or tender.

Serve as an accompaniment to a protein or eat the veggies as an entrée. Enjoy!

ELEVEN

Reviewing My Script

In many ways Natasha is a miniature Candace. Like me she is interested in acting and enjoys sitting on the set for hours on end soaking in all that she sees. They say she also looks a lot like me with her long blonde hair and big blue eyes, but when I see her with Val, I see much of him in there too.

One moment she can hang with the boys and get dirty without thought, and the next she's wearing my heels around the house. I'm not quite ready to let the heels move past our front door yet. Once I did break the rule, letting her wear my wedge sandals to the Third Street Promenade (Can you believe we're the same shoe size?), but after two opinionated women gave us the "look," I thought it might be best to keep them at home for a bit. The world isn't ready for that just yet. Neither are we.

Natasha is acting now too. She goes on auditions and has done three commercials so far. One for Best Friends Club dolls, the Littlest Pet Shop, and the other was for Whimsy stuffed animals. I know she's a good actress and is enjoying the process like I did.

I remember one of my first commercials for KFC. My lines were "Ooooh" and "Ahhhhh," but Mom coached me for hours, ensuring that I said them just right. It wasn't a matter of simply saying the words; she also taught me to make my eyes sparkle.

I did about twenty-five commercials before my days on *Full House*, which included one for Cabbage Patch Babies. I had a few more lines to recite for that one, but the reason I even got the commercial in the first place was because of the endearing way I looked at those dolls. They were the most beautiful babies to me, and I swear they were real. I held them like the real thing and believed every word that I spoke. "Goodness, it's past your nap time," I said, before drifting off to sleep with my Cabbage Patch doll.

I'm definitely excited for Natasha, but I'm cautious in reviewing the materials before she goes on any audition. We're given a portion of the script, which is known in the industry as "sides," and if the sides don't look good to us, the part isn't an option. For one job the sides looked fine, but once we were able to read the entire script, we passed on the audition. I see her talent, but it's our job as parents to guide and protect her rather than compromise merely because it's something she wants.

I coach her before all the auditions, and I think it's a great way to connect as mother and daughter, actor and coach.

Like her brothers, she is a leader with a strong personality that sometimes gets the best of her. She's incredibly outgoing, and like her smile her personality is big in every way. She stands on her principles to get what she wants or what she thinks she might need. I know when she's older this will be an advantage for her walk with Christ, but as a parent, I have to direct her until that time comes.

I stand in faith on Proverbs 22:6, "Train a child in the way he should go, and when he is old he will not turn from it."

Natasha is at the threshold of womanhood. She's beginning to make choices for herself, and a little too often a bit of that preteen attitude starts to emerge. If left unchecked, it could grow, and so at this stage of her life, I have to stay closely connected in order to be a leader and guide her. As her guide I need to be watchful at all times.

If I tell her to hang her sweater in the closet after school and also to tuck her running shoes inside, I may get results, or I may find a running shoe lying nearby in the hall. But when I create a checklist for the kids so they know that they are being monitored, I find they make a conscious effort to improve.

It's a simple human response. Basic psychology teaches us that monitored behavior equals improved behavior. Have you ever tried typing when someone is looking over your shoulder? We tend to trip up because we become overconscious of our actions—another response to monitored behavior.

How does this relate to staying healthy and fit? Monitored living brings us into the all-important state of conscious living, and conscious living ensures that we get the job done. When we are mindful of our actions, we start to realize the excess that we eat. When we are alert, we are better equipped to handle temptation. When we are prepared, we are more likely to stick to a wise eating and exercise plan.

Webster's Dictionary defines the word *conscious* this way: "acting with critical awareness, as in 'a conscious effort to do better.'"

Now let's consider the characteristics of conscious living from a biblical perspective:

- Conscious living involves choice. God calls for us to make a choice either to serve Him or not. As for me and my house, we will serve the Lord.
- Conscious living involves determination. We are instructed to work as unto the Lord and not for man. That includes me. I live healthy because my body is the temple of the Holy Spirit, through which I can glorify God.
- Conscious living involves accountability. Nothing is hidden from the eyes of God. One day we will give account for every action we've done and every word we have spoken

To discover how conscious you're living, consider the following:

- Do you eat mindlessly, or do you consider the food you consume?
- Do you channel surf, or do you turn the TV on to watch a program, and then turn it off when it's over?
- Do you walk the aisles of the grocery store buying whatever looks good, or do you make a list and follow it?
- Do you listen as much as you talk?
- When you read, does your mind wander off?
- Do you surf the Internet, and later realize you just wasted a whole lot of time?
- Do you have a closet full of clothing that you bought on a whim?
- Look around the room. Do you see things that you constantly step over instead of putting them in their place?

If you find that you're zoning out of life a little too often, this may be a good time to start monitoring yourself and start living again.

It's often suggested to dieters that they begin to journal their food intake. If you've ever wondered why that is, here is your answer—to bring us into a mindful state of living where we purpose to live out our plan.

Grab a pen and a paper right now. Got it? Good! Now mark down what you ate so far today. Had coffee in the morning? Don't forget to record the amount of sugar you added. A spot of cream? Record that too. We don't need to get too specific about this with measuring and weighing our food; it's just so you get a general idea of where you're improving or where you desperately need to change. As the day moves along, keep a record of all the food and beverages you consume, including water. I'd suggest that this journal be specifically for this purpose and that you consider it an accountability partner.

You can also record your Bible reading. What would a healthy diet be like without daily nourishment from the Word of God? "The fear of the LORD is pure, enduring forever. The ordinances of the LORD are sure and altogether righteous. They are more precious than gold, than much pure gold; they are sweeter than honey, than honey from the comb." (Ps. 19:9–10)

After losing fourteen pounds, Bonnie shared that she was on a plateau for three weeks straight. She continued to eat well and work out at the gym six days a week, but the needle on the scale wouldn't budge until her *spiritual* eating plan changed. Digging into the Word every single morning over the following two weeks, she lost seven more pounds. Coincidence? No, actually, it's not. It's a result of conscious living. Through fellowship with God, Bonnie became further determined and conscious of her actions. She realized she was drinking too many calories, going a little heavy on the dressing at times, and having a few too many rewards. Most importantly she discovered that fellowship with God was satisfying her craving for food. Meditation on the Word gave her the clarity and strength she needed to change while God was transforming her desires.

When we become conscious with God through Bible reading, Scripture meditation, and prayer, we clarify our purpose and draw from His strength. That's so important in every stage of our journey, whether we're just starting out or have been walking for years.

Just like our children, our bodies need mindful discipleship. That's where the Spirit becomes a parent of sorts. Parents go through three stages of training:

1. Leading the way.
2. Walking beside them.
3. Walking behind them.

In the first stage we lead the way, live by example, and set clear guidelines for them. My boys are in this stage. Young minds hungry to be filled with knowledge, watching eyes looking for examples to follow. In the same manner our bodies require that first stage of training when we set out on new paths. We need people around us who are good examples to follow, and we need clear guidelines to adhere to so we know what to do. This is the stage in which we closely monitor ourselves and remain mindful of our actions.

Natasha is nearing the second stage where I'll soon be walking beside her. While the boys are still in the first stage, I know that in just a few short years she'll be a young woman with a mind of her own. I pray that I have been a good example thus far and that I've instilled good values in her. She'll be making more choices, and trust will have to kick in when she's out of my sight. The same holds true for us. There comes a time when the plan we choose becomes ingrained in us. That's when the conscious living that we chose becomes habit, conviction, and routine. It's a comforting phase to walk in because we're living a lifestyle instead of an outline of rules. We instinctively follow because our hearts have been trained.

The third stage is a place of freedom. That's when our children are adults, making their own decisions and living their lives. My kids are not there yet. But I know that when the time comes, I'll still be a part of their lives, only my job as a mom will be to stand behind them and catch them if they fall.

You will reach that place of freedom too, and persistence will be there to catch you if you fall. God will be there when you fall, but I also know that He equips us with persistence, which is the very thing we need to move on. We all fall, but persistence tells us to get up and get moving again. I slip up from time to time when I eat more than I should or skip workouts, but I've matured in this area so that I know I can get right back on track today and trust that I'll stay on track tomorrow. I haven't always been this way. Remember I was the kid with the chipmunk cheeks eating Big Macs before each audition. I was the young woman turning to food when Val was out playing hockey. I struggled immensely, and I praise God that I did because I learned, and I grew, and I gleaned faith in the process.

If you're just entering that first stage of your journey, rejoice knowing that you will grow and that with maturity and time it will get easier. You'll be able to walk into a restaurant and not only know what item to choose off the menu, you will want to make the best choice and will enjoy every bite.

I've gotten to the point in my own life where I eat until I'm satisfied. Not only do I not desire to eat more, but my stomach isn't the size that it used to be so I can't. Conscious training has transformed me into a different person spiritually, mentally, and physically.

I hope you grabbed that pen and are starting to record your progress. You'll find that keeping a food diary is a helpful way to keep track of your changes. We can see our progression as well as where we've gone wrong. And in addition to Bible reading, I also see the value in keeping a diary/journal of all the times you've heard God speaking to you. You may be reading Scripture and something pops out to you, or a sermon on the radio seems to be speaking directly to you. It could be answers to prayer (I like to write down my prayer requests and check them off as they're answered) or unexpected encouragement from a friend. Any number of things could be God's way of speaking to you.

A food diary and a God journal go hand in hand perfectly! Keep track of what you're eating, how much you're exercising, and how much water you drink. Next, write down the moments you know God was encouraging you along the way, no matter how small they seem. When I really start to notice God's hand in every aspect of daily living—accepting that it's not just a coincidence—I'm empowered to press on. It could be through something as simple as a TV commercial. I might be driving by a gym and be reminded to exercise. It could be a delicious recipe on your computer that offers a better alternative for a healthy dinner instead of going to the drive-through window. When you start recording each event, you'll be amazed at how active God really is in your life. Consider them as an encouraging nudge from the Lord.

God is coaching me every step of the way. It's a great way to connect as Father and daughter, actor and coach. Sometimes the "sides" look fine, but because He's reviewing the entire script of my life, I know that He knows what's best. "Father knows best."

> "The LORD disciplines those he loves, as a father the son he delights in." (Prov. 3:12)

The Pantry

CHOCKED-FULL OF FOOD FOR THOUGHT

The Main Ingredient

Whether our actions are an asset or a liability, conscious living brings us to a place where we take note of them. By being aware of our weakness, we can change our behavior to strengthen our resolve or do away with bad habits. When we see the good that we've done and the difference it's making, we are able to note the area of growth and improve upon it. Closely monitoring ourselves is one way to bring conscious living to the forefront and make the changes that need to be made.

A Slice of Advice

Dear Candace,

I love what you're doing and think you look amazingly beautiful! Full House is still one of my favorite shows! They just don't make them like that anymore—good clean fun!

I checked out your Web site and was reading this question and answer column when I came across the answer to your secret for keeping fit! First time I'm hearing of Pilates (strange pronunciation to boot!). I looked it up on Wikipedia and found it grouped with yoga. A lot of things said against doing yoga, so I was wondering whether Pilates would fall into the same group. What are your thoughts on yoga too?
—Bella

Dear Bella,

Great question! I tried yoga on and off about nine and ten years ago but always felt uncomfortable with the meditation. I loved holding the positions as they strengthen your body immensely but could never put my finger on the thing I didn't like about it. Over the years I too have read several articles on yoga and the spiritual dangers of it. I decided to stay away from it although I'm not saying it's wrong to do it by any means; it's just my preference. Pilates on the other hand does not fit into the same category. It is not about meditation and contacting your "inner self." It is strictly movements done on either a mat, a reformer, a chair or tower that all work to strengthen your core, resulting in long, lean muscles. It's amazing and the best workout I've ever done. I never thought I'd have a flat stomach after having three kids, but I do! Oh, and the breathing is important only so your core is working properly— not for spiritual reasons.

—Candace

A Pinch of Practicality

Close yourself in with God by giving Him your full attention during times of prayer. Rather than spilling off a few words as you drift off to sleep, choose your prayer time to take place during peak hours of the day. Do you find that you're most alert at 11:00 a.m.? If so, that might be a good time to sneak away to a quiet corner for prayer.

Many people find that kneeling to pray helps them focus and is an act of reverence to God. This may not be ideal for the office, but when you are at home, the foot of the bed doubles well as a mercy seat. Ask God to be with you on your journey to reshaping your body, spirit, and soul. Not merely as a walking buddy, but rather as one who leads the way. Make it a daily routine to meet with Him in prayer to discuss your ups and downs.

Food for Thought

- Train a child in the way he should go, and when he is old he will not turn from it. (Prov. 22:6)
- The fear of the LORD is pure,
  enduring forever.
  The ordinances of the LORD are sure
  and altogether righteous. They are more precious than gold, than much pure gold;
  they are sweeter than honey,
  than honey from the comb. (Ps. 19:9–10)
- The LORD disciplines those he loves, as a father the son he delights in. (Prov. 3:12)

The Candy Dish

Every act of conscious learning requires the willingness to suffer an injury to one's self-esteem. That is why young children, before they are aware of their own self-importance, learn so easily. —Thomas S. Szasz

Yogurt Parfait

Serves 4

INGREDIENTS

3 cups vanilla nonfat yogurt
1 cup fresh strawberries
1 pint fresh blackberries, raspberries, or blueberries
1 cup good quality granola

DIRECTIONS

In a small bowl, combine strawberries with fresh berries.

Layer ⅓ cup vanilla yogurt into the bottom each of four wide glasses or dessert bowls.

Alternate layers of fruit and granola with yogurt until glasses are filled to the top. Serve parfaits immediately, so that the granola stays crunchy.

Makes for a refreshing treat on a warm afternoon!

TWELVE

Life Is a Glass Jar

Friends are often taken aback when I describe an average day to them. I wake at 3:45 a.m., wash and blow-dry my hair, and take the dog out for a quick walk so I can leave by 4:30 to be on set at *Make It or Break It,* by 5:30. I sit in the makeup and hair chair for the next hour and a half, where I multitask by going over my lines and having a quick bite to eat, and then I'm off to wardrobe.

I'm on set at 7:00 a.m. for rehearsal. At 7:15, when the rest of the country is starting to wake from their slumber, I'm back in the makeup and hair trailer getting touched up again while Tom from the sound department is professionally hiding a mic pack onto the back of my bra. We start shooting by 7:30, and depending on how many scenes I'm in, I might be finished by 10:00 a.m. or 8 p.m.

If I'm finished by 2:00, I rush over to school to pick up my three kids. I know that Val could pick them up too, but I really enjoy that time we spend together, hearing about their day and telling them about mine. I grew up in a home where my mom and dad were involved in our lives, and I want the same for my kids today. My mom always came to the set and baked her famous Chocolate Chip Lace cookies for the *Full House* cast and crew on Friday tape nights. Unfortunately I can't share that recipe, since it's a Cameron family secret, but let me just say, my mom is well liked!

At 3:45 we have a snack, and I help with homework. Then Maks, Lev, and I hop into the car at 4:30 to head out to hockey. Yeah, you read that right—hockey. Knowing how many bruises, cuts, and scuffs you can get, Val and I weren't too excited about the boys embracing the Bures' passion for hockey. But seeing how much Maks and Lev love the sport, we couldn't hold them back. So, just as I did for my husband, I go to the games and cheer the boys on. You might call it screaming when you see me in the stands, but what can I say? Those are my kids on the ice! Hockey practice also gives me a chance to open my laptop, return e-mails, work on my Bible study homework, and make phone calls to my managers and publicist. I try to multitask and use that hour and a half wisely.

Praise God for a husband who likes to make dinner and does it so well because once hockey is done we're tired and ready to eat.

By 8:30 I put the kids to bed and start learning my lines for the next morning's scenes. That's a typical day for me unless I add travel to the mix like today; then of course things can get even busier. As a matter of fact, I just stepped off a plane in San Francisco, and minutes later I'm writing this chapter.

Am I complaining? Not a chance! My workweek is great. I'm part of an exciting show, and I still have plenty of time for my family.

I'm often asked questions like:

- How do you do it, being a mom, involved with your family— how do you keep up?

- How do you ensure that God is always number one in your life?
- How do you maintain a career, a family, and still find time to work out?
- How do you find time to get involved at school?
- How do you do it all and still have time to wash and condition your hair?!

My answer is simple: prioritize.

You might have heard the story of the high school teacher who placed a glass gallon jar in front of his students. After filling the jar with large stones, he asked the class, "Is the jar full?" Unanimously the class said yes.

The teacher then took a bag he had sitting on the counter beside him and poured gravel into the jar. Together they watched it slide into the empty spaces.

"Now I'll ask you again," he said. "Is it full?"

This time some students said yes while others said no.

Scooping sand from a bucket below him, the teacher added sand to the mixture, lifting and shaking the jar until the grains settled in.

"Is it full?" he smiled, wondering if they had finally caught on.

Together the class shouted, "No!"

Grabbing a pitcher of water from his desk, the teacher topped off the mixture and tightened the lid.

"Now, can anyone tell me what this object lesson reflects?" He asked looking out at the class.

One student said that regardless of how busy our lives are we can always make time for more stuff, while another joked that the stones were his dinner, the sand was dessert, and the water was a soda to wash it all down. But the real answer came from a boy in the front row who noticed the order that the objects went in.

He said, "If we prioritize our lives to take care of the important things first, everything finds and settles into its place, so everything can get done."

My life is like that jar. God and family are the precious stones that I place into the jar first. They are my number one priority. Because I know that putting my husband first and taking care of my children are pleasing to God, I know that I serve the Lord when I serve my family.

But don't let all of this talk lead you to think I'm a spiritual giant. There are days when I don't read my Bible (I hate to admit that), and there are days I'm off and running without starting out in prayer. But it doesn't take long for it all to catch up to me because of the emptiness I feel when I don't give myself to the Lord first thing each day.

When you have truly trusted in Christ and are walking in obedience, you have a sense of peace, joy, comfort, and love that you just can't get anywhere else. When you see God in all His glory, speaking to you, directing you, performing miracles in your everyday life, you can't help but want that relationship with Him every single day. The thought of not hearing God's voice because I'm not listening or I'm not in tune with Him makes me crazy!

It takes work, it takes diligence, and it takes commitment. But in order to accomplish everything, I have to keep my priorities in order and fill my jar with precious stones first.

How important is God to you? If you feel the void when you don't pray or read your Bible, that's good! But it shouldn't be out of guilt, and it never is for me. I spend time with God out of an utmost heartfelt gratitude that I have for Him because of His love in His sacrificial death for me.

We all need a little encouragement along the way to remind us what those priorities are. That's why it's so important to have friends around that are walking the same walk, keeping us accountable, and giving us support. I don't know what I'd do without my weekly Bible study girlfriends!

This intimate group has met at my house for the past seven years. We pray with and for each other and work through an organized Bible study from someone like Beth Moore or Priscilla Shirer, two of my favorite Bible teachers! I trust this group. Knowing that what is said in the group stays in the group allows us to be real in our quest to learn, understand, and apply biblical teaching to our daily lives. It's safe to say this small group has been the biggest asset for my growth and walk with the Lord.

I try to keep my eyes focused on the Lord and not on the world. It's easy for me when I'm faced with a decision to ask God, "Would this choice be pleasing to You?" Praying over it and holding it up to Scripture helps keep me from letting the world get in the way. His guidance helps remind me that faith and family come first, and all else is second.

The reason priorities have been so important through my journey is because while I've been fortifying my body with diet and exercise, I also know that fortifying the very core of my being powers the actions I take.

Could I get out of bed at 3:45 without self-control? Could I balance it all without patience? Could I enjoy every stage of my children's lives without joy? And what would my future hold without faith?

You start living the best life you can, taking the steps you know you should take, but then the familiar voice whispers in your ear, before it moves through your lips, "I've tried and I've failed. I can't possibly succeed." That's exactly the kind of discouragement that keeps us out of the race.

You were running a good race. Who cut in on you and kept you from obeying the truth? (Gal. 5:7)

We start running the race with joyful enthusiasm, having faith that this time we will kick the bad habits—this time we will make it work! But then someone cuts in on our dance with the Lord and leads us away. Don't let him whisper for even a moment. Anything that is contrary to the fruit of the Spirit will lead us farther and farther away from the prize. That includes impatience, lack of self-control, and irritability among several other bad-apple thoughts that attempt to creep in.

> *That kind of persuasion does not come from the one who calls you. "A little yeast works through the whole batch of dough."* (Gal. 5:8–9)

Paul was talking to the Galatians here, admonishing those hoping to be justified by the law, thinking that law and grace should be mixed. But the verses also speak to those of us today, who struggle to walk by the Spirit with one foot in the flesh.

We're born with a sinful nature, prone to crave the things of the world by the lust of the flesh. Just looking around us, we can see that addictions are rampant, whether that addiction is to alcohol, smoking, sex, gambling, pornography or—this one might sound familiar—overeating. There's hardly a person you'll meet who hasn't struggled in one way or another to release the hold they have on this world. But the good news is that the world doesn't and will not have a hold on us! If we walk by the Spirit, we are free from the law of sin and death.

> *So I say, live by the Spirit, and you will not gratify the desires of the sinful nature.* (Gal. 5:16)

How? Good question, but I also have a good answer! Most of us know that the Spirit lives in us, but the question remains: How does that Spirit help us give up our strongholds? What is the link between Spirit and freedom?

Here is the answer: The Spirit helps us desire the things that are contrary to this world. He influences our actions, our thoughts, and our passions when we let Him move in. I mean really move in—unpack His bags and even rearrange the furniture if He wants to—not as a guest but as a resident.

When I struggled with bulimia during those early years of marriage, I was more concerned about being a good person than I was about my relationship with Christ. The freedom that was possible hadn't clicked for me until I came to a full understanding of God's saving grace. That's when I desired a relationship with Him, and allowed the Holy Spirit to move into my life.

My priorities were off. The jar was so full of gravel and sand that the most precious stone I owned didn't fit. That stone is the rock of my salvation, Jesus Christ. It wasn't until I emptied myself and put Jesus in first that I began to feel empowered again by His Spirit.

Mark this verse in your heart:

> *For the sinful nature desires what is contrary to the Spirit, and*
> *the Spirit what is contrary to the sinful nature. (Gal 5:17)*

Can you imagine what that's like, to desire the things of God so much that your appetite for this world fades away? That's the power of the Holy Spirit and the fruit that He brings. Spiritual fruit doesn't just help us smile on Sundays. It's found in the love we have for our boss Monday morning. It's the joy we discover when we leave our purse on the park bench. It's the peace we find when we're stuck bumper to bumper in rush-hour traffic, and the self-control we exhibit when we're at a buffet.

Hebrews 12:1–2 says, "Let us throw off everything that hinders and the sin that so easily entangles, and let us run with perseverance the race marked out for us. Let us fix our eyes on Jesus, the author and perfecter of our faith, who for the joy set before him endured the cross, scorning its shame, and sat down at the right hand of the throne of God."

What a powerful verse! "Run with *perseverance*." That word is tucked in there barely noticed but so important when we choose to live well.

Consider the following:

- Have you ever given up on a diet because you weren't seeing the results you wanted, only to look back later and wish that you hadn't given up?
- Have you ever joined a gym, bought a treadmill, or started a home exercise program but quit when the going got tough?
- Have you ever started with a commitment to read the Bible every single night but gave up because you lost interest?
- Have you ever given up on a marriage because he wasn't fulfilling your needs and desires?

Most of us will answer yes to at least one of these questions, and as a result most of us have missed out on a blessing that comes with staying the course.

I've come to see the value in staying the course with each mountain I climb. Not only am I building stamina with each obstacle I overcome; I'm also learning to lean on God with each step I take.

Your life is a jar, empty and ready to fill. What will you place in it first?

The Pantry
CHOCKED-FULL OF FOOD FOR THOUGHT

The Main Ingredient

Eating healthy and staying fit will take a little effort on your part, but where do you find the time? There is time for everything if everything is done in order of importance. If you find that you don't have the time to exercise, examine yourself to see how important it really is to you. Do you need to move your level of commitment up a notch? Same goes with Bible reading or spending time with your family. Organize your to-do list according to what needs doing first to ensure it gets done. The less important things will fall into place accordingly.

A Slice of Advice

Dear Candace,

Hi! I just read a weight-loss question you answered and wondered, What did you mean by "giving your food issues up to God."

I am a married mother of four, and I am having such a hard time! (I am on Weight Watchers.)
—Anne

Dear Anne,

By "food issues" I meant some unhealthy eating habits I'd acquired in the past. For me, the only way to get past my abuse with food was getting serious about it with God. I needed to constantly pray that I'd stay away from unhealthy alternatives and that I'd eat right and exercise instead.

This sin was one that I loved and didn't want to give up. I was scared. I constantly wrestled with it. And I knew it was keeping me from a closer relationship with God and that I had to give it over to Him.

I said to Him, "I can't do this on my own. I'm willing to take a step in faith to stop doing it the wrong way, knowing with all my heart that You will provide me the willpower to say 'no' or give me a way out."

That was the last time I was ever going to pray it. I didn't want that struggle for the rest of my life. And while my view of food is not problem for me anymore, it's an area I always have to keep close at heart and pray about. I know the enemy is lurking, waiting at the door to creep in.

I think going on a diet like Weight Watchers is great to learn portion control and to retrain yourself to eat properly. Food is a hard battle for most American's since we have such abundance and it's so readily available to us. Stick to a plan and keep God close by your side.
—Candace

A Pinch of Practicality

A great way to ensure that everything gets done is to make a list of your daily activities first thing each morning. Then before you dig in, prioritize the list. When ordering your list, consider the following three suggestions:

1. Ask yourself if any of these things are on a tight deadline. If you know that something is due that day or the next, you'll need to ensure it's near the top of your list.
2. Consider if any are stressing you out. If something is weighing on your mind day after day, get it out of the way. Procrastinating on these will just bring added stress. You may want to put this somewhere in the middle of your list, meaning it doesn't *have* to be done, but it should.

3. Decide which activities benefit your spirit and health. Ensure that those things are near the top of your list. Taking care of yourself will give you the energy and wisdom to take care of the rest.

Food for Thought

A recap of Scripture to meditate on:

- You were running a good race. Who cut in on you and kept you from obeying the truth? (Gal. 5:7)
- That kind of persuasion does not come from the one who calls you. "A little yeast works through the whole batch of dough." (Gal. 5:8–9)
- So I say, live by the Spirit, and you will not gratify the desires of the sinful nature. (Gal. 5:16)
- For the sinful nature desires what is contrary to the Spirit, and the Spirit what is contrary to the sinful nature. (Gal. 5:17)
- Let us throw off everything that hinders and the sin that so easily entangles, and let us run with perseverance the race marked out for us. Let us fix our eyes on Jesus, the author and perfecter of our faith, who for the joy set before him endured the cross, scorning its shame, and sat down at the right hand of the throne of God. (Heb. 12:1–2)

The Candy Dish

Set priorities for your goals. A major part of successful living lies in the ability to put first things first. Indeed, the reason most major goals are not achieved is that we spend our time doing second things first. —Author Unknown

Black Bean Pineapple Enchiladas

Makes 10 to 12 enchiladas

INGREDIENTS

1 red bell pepper
½ medium white or yellow onion: chopped
1 tablespoon olive oil
1 15 oz can of black beans, drained
1 20 oz can of crushed pineapple in pineapple juice
1 rotisserie chicken
Cilantro (optional)
1 cup Mexican shredded cheese
1 large can of enchilada sauce
10 to 12 medium-size multigrain flour tortillas

DIRECTIONS

Dice the red bell pepper and onion and sauté in olive oil over medium heat or until tender. Add drained black beans and pineapple including juice into the skillet.

Stir and heat. Pull apart white meat chicken and shred. Add chicken to the skillet and cook till hot.

Two, 9 x 13 glass or casserole dishes

Lay one tortilla in the dish and scoop approximately ½ cup filling into tortilla filling the center end to end. Tuck 2 edges of the tortilla over and roll the untucked side completely enclosing the filling. Place seam-side down in dish. Stuff and roll the rest of the tortillas the same way until dish is full. Pour the enchilada sauce over the top and sprinkle cheese on top.

Bake at 350 degrees for 15 minutes until bubbly hot.

THIRTEEN

Discover Contentment

Mandy is the only person on Earth with Mandy Young's Disease. She's also the only person on Earth who can brighten a room in three seconds flat with one flash of her smile, and I'm blessed to call her my friend. She's a medical phenomenon with a gene mutation technically named "Irak4 Gene Defect," by which her body forms its own infection. Although her body doesn't show normal symptoms, when it finally does show the slightest sign of trouble, she is on her deathbed.

At nine years old, Mandy lost her leg. Two rare infections set in, and the combination of both was the first doctors had seen since World War II. This life-threatening time of her life was devastating, and it's also the very thing that brought her into my world.

My brother Kirk and his fiancée Chelsea were sent to the hospital through Make a Wish Foundation to visit sick children and brighten their day. Mandy had been discharged about a week earlier, but when Kirk and Chelsea heard Mandy's incredible story, they knew that they had to call her back in for a visit.

Assuming it was a routine appointment with another doctor or two, Mandy had no idea who she was about to meet. A crowd of doctors, nurses, and hospital staff stood before her as she was wheeled down the hall. And it wasn't until the crowd parted like the Red Sea that she realized just who she was going to meet. One look at the two of them, and she immediately knew it was "Mike Seaver" and "Kate" of *Growing Pains* fame. That one-of-a-kind smile of hers lit up the hall.

Kirk meets with hundreds of sick children per year. He and Chelsea choose six or seven of those children each summer to go to Camp Firefly with their families to camp with his. Back in those days when I was still living at home with Mom, Dad, Bridgette, Melissa and Kirk, our entire family would head out to the camp for the week. That's where I met Mandy, her sister Alex, their mother Lisa, and father Speed.

My mom also called inviting them to come out to LA for an entire week. They were able to meet the casts of both *Full House* and *Growing Pains* and watch the shows tape. I was about twelve years old that year when we fell in love with their family, and over time we've done our best to all keep in touch.

When I was about fifteen years old, *Full House* went to Disney World, taping the episode in Orlando, Florida. The Youngs met us there for a few days, and we all connected again. Lisa took over my fan club for a while, sending out photos and opening mail, so she'd have something to do while Mandy was in isolation. But over the years, keeping in touch became more of a Christmas card back and forth than anything else.

Fast-forward to fourteen years later when I started speaking at churches all over the country.

Lisa said, "I heard you will be speaking near us. Can we come?"

I was excited to reconnect. When Lisa and Mandy arrived, it was one of those God moments. I had so many speaking engagements in that area over the next six months and was eager to see them each time. After every event, I rushed back to my table where CDs of my testimony, faith-based T-shirts, and 8x10 color photos were available, so Lisa and Mandy started helping me out while I took care of autographs. This was great. I needed someone to travel with me, and they wanted the job. So for the past four years, Lisa, Mandy, and sometimes Alex travel with me, taking care of all the details so I can concentrate on sharing my story.

Lisa is like my mom away from home, which is nice to have when I travel, but the funny thing is that she's deathly afraid of flying. She gets on an airplane to be with me, which is a huge deal for her, but nevertheless, she does.

One particular weekend we flew in a tiny plane into a small city. Despite the fact that I fly a lot, it was one of the worst flights of both of our lives. I couldn't help but laugh the entire time, watching Lisa white knuckle the armrest, and practice what looked like lamaze. I was laughing out loud. It was hysterical! (Hysterically terrifying if you ask Lisa.)

Lisa and Mandy have been great travel companions both on the road and through this walk I call faith. Mandy has faced adversity time and time again with a smile on her face that even PMS at its worst wouldn't dare to remove. Loving life at its fullest, she says: "I have led a life that most might not find enjoyable, but I love my life, and I wouldn't change a thing. God has truly blessed me. I sometimes just have to remind myself that God only gives me what I can handle and that what doesn't kill me will only make me stronger." Mandy and people like her remind me that the journey through life, with all its adversity, is one to be enjoyed. People like

Mandy don't say, "If I only had my leg . . ." They replace trials with smiles and choose to live in contentment.

We can start enjoying life by putting aside the "ifs" today:

- I'd be happier if this house was bigger.
- I'd be happier if my stomach was tighter.
- I'd be happier if only I could wear a size 6 again.

Now let's put the "buts" aside too:

- I have a great marriage, but my husband doesn't take me out enough.
- My kids are wonderful, but my two-year-old is going through a phase right now.
- I used to spend time with the Lord, but lately I'm just swamped for time.

As he thinks in his heart, so is he. (Prov. 23:7 NKJV)

Don't think for a minute that the discouragement you wear in your heart won't show on your face. Happiness is one cosmetic that's God given and free for all. I want it, don't you? Of course, we all do! I'd love to wear a smile 24-7, even 48-7 if that were possible, but even more than happiness itself, I strive to be content, living in the true joy with the peaceful knowledge that God is in control, for "godliness with contentment is great gain" (1 Tim. 6:6).

Yes, I still have hopes and dreams that will point me in one direction or the other, but ultimately when I lay my desire on the altar of worship where I trust God for my life, I'll allow God's grace to power each step. That's what contentment does, and it's learned by patience and practice. The apostle Paul said, "For I have learned, in whatsoever state I am, therewith to be content" (Phil. 4:11 KJV).

Let's look at five ways to find contentment in your life today:

1. **Stop looking back**. Remember Lot's wife—otherwise known as the pillar of salt? One can only praise God that we're not in her shoes because so many of us have looked back a thousand times more than we should have.

Longing for the things of the past or the things of the future is our way of saying, "I'm not content with what I have," or "I don't trust God with my future." Sodom was a sinful and corrupt place to be, and yet for lack of faith, Lot's wife looked back. Some of us have done the same as we've looked back on our past, wishing we could just pick and choose certain things that we lost—like that twenty-three-inch waist, or skin so tight it snapped into place. Others look to the future with anxiety, praying that God will open doors, clarify their path, give them direction, and make them skinny—today. The praying is great, but the problem too often is that we fail to leave the anxiety there, and we carry it with us instead. It's like taking a trip to the cleaners and then hauling your dirty laundry back home. Doesn't make much sense when you consider how fruitless it is.

By watching people like Mandy, I've come to learn that true contentment is when I can say, "I bring my petitions to you, Lord. I lay them at Your feet and trust that Your direction is best for my life," with the faith to stand by those words.

Peter wisely guides us on the path to contentment when he writes, "Cast all your anxiety on him because he cares for you" (1 Pet. 5:7).

2. **Count your blessings.** Is it quiet in the room? I hope so because I want you to pause and consider your blessings before you move on. Discouragement is a roadblock that too many of us are staring at, hoping that someone will shove it out of the way so we can move on with our journey.

Live outward instead of living an inward-focused life. We accomplish this by letting go of the "I wants" for a focus on the "I haves."

Look back. I know I said not to, but I'm making an exception this once. I want you to look back and witness the fact that God is faithful. He has brought you this far, and He isn't about to leave you where you are today. "'For I know the plans I have for you,' declares the Lord, 'plans to prosper you and not to harm you, plans to give you hope and a future'" (Jer. 29:11).

Let's start counting those blessings now . . . Do you have children? A wonderful husband? A pantry full of food? A best friend? A good income? A talent? Sunshine on your face? Great cheekbones? Kind parents? Long healthy hair? Whatever you can praise God for, do it right now. Go into a room by yourself if you need to, but release your discouragement by receiving the encouragement we find when we dwell on our blessings. Name them as you give thanks to the Lord. That's when you'll get past the roadblock and move on in your faith.

> *"Taste and see that the LORD is good; blessed is the man who takes refuge in him." (Ps. 34:8)* Amen!

3. **Delight in the Lord.** *Webster's Dictionary* defines *delight* this way: "A high degree of gratification, extreme pleasure."

Have you ever met a hard-core hockey fan? I mean someone who really delights in the sport? I've seen hockey fans who invest in season tickets, attend every home game, buy their favorite player's jerseys and wait for hours, game after game, just to get it signed. They know all the stats of their team's players along with those of nearly every other player in the league. They buy all of the team paraphernalia they can get their hands on to reflect a devotion to their team—coffee cups, bumper stickers, license plates. You name it—they have it! These fans attend all of the team's charitable events. They watch multiple games simultaneously on television, stay up for hockey highlights, and play hockey video games in between. A serious fan will keep a stick and roller hockey puck in his car so he can play at any spare moment, or he'll join a league of his own that wakes him up in the wee hours of the morning or keeps him up way too late just so he gets some ice time. Lastly, and with rare exception, the serious hockey fan plans all vacation time around the playoffs.

Can I define *delight* any better than that? It would be tough, unless I started in about my passion for fashion, but let's not go there today.

With that said, I'll ask, "Do you truly delight in the Lord?" Do you seek to include Him in all that you do, or is He just a channel that you turn to every now and then?

I hope you've discovered and continue to discover the joy that flows when you delight in fellowship with the Lord. It may take a bit of slowing down on your part to see it, but His glory is evident in our world. It's there to touch and to hold and delight in. Read a psalm, watch the rain fall, take a walk and chat with Him, watch the clouds float by, hold a newborn, play with a ladybug, give a gift in His name, feel a breeze on your face, listen to the sound of laughter, taste a chocolate melting on your tongue, enjoy the smell of your husband, watch a seed sprout in soil. Discover Him in all that you do. And when you're not discovering Him, seek Him out because when you do you'll find Him. Seek Him and praise Him for all that He is, for God delights in the praise of His people!

> "Delight yourself in the LORD, and he will give you the desires of your heart." (Ps. 37:4)

4. **Embrace the recipe that you own.** I'm going to go out on a limb and be stereotypical for a moment by saying that women—at least the ones I've met—have a tendency to compare themselves with others. Dare I also say often? You may not be the wealthiest, the thinnest, or the most attractive person you know—neither am I. But it's also likely that there are less attractive, less successful, and

less fortunate people too. That's why it's pointless even to begin to measure ourselves against others. It's a fact of life. There will always be prettier, thinner, and more successful women than us, but that's okay. Let's accept this fact and move on. Among the glitter and glitz of Hollywood, there is one thing that it doesn't possess, and that, my dear, is you. Embrace that.

There will never be another woman who owns the look, the personality, and the experience that you do. Those ingredients make up the recipe that defines who you are, and it's your gift from the Lord—own it. Originality is something to be desired, and you've got it, girl, whether you know it or not.

5. **Choose your reaction.** After losing her leg, Mandy was in a coma for weeks on end. They didn't know if she was going to live or die and were initially told she had a 3 percent chance of survival. She didn't even know that her leg was missing, and when she did wake up, how would they tell her?

Lisa remembers the nurse waking them up in the hospital to say that Mandy was finally awake. It was a miracle moment. They decided then and there to be honest with her. It was amputation and life or saving her leg only to let her move on from this life—an option they didn't feel was in line with God's plan. He had a special purpose for her life, and they wanted to see her live that life out.

"We will get through this," they said, "together."

It was the Fourth of July. Mandy was still recovering in the hospital, and while Speed was by her side, Lisa went home to take care of some things. Opening the closet door, she looked down at each little shoe, lined up side by side, then took the left shoe away from each pair they owned. At that moment Lisa realized their lives were forever changed. It was also a time when she realized that she needed to prove to her daughter that life could be the same.

When Mandy got home from the hospital, she was expected to make her bed just as she always had. "But I can't," she cried, moving around on one leg.

Lisa insisted she could and then went off to her bedroom to cry. It was the only way they knew how to have a sense of normalcy. They knew that life would be hard, but they chose to live life just as they always had on the strong foundation of faith.

"That's the life we've been given to live," Lisa says with a smile, "and despite our affliction we've chosen joy over sorrow. "

I'd like to encourage you to consider your reaction the next time you feel a blow. Forgot your keys? Late for a meeting? Didn't get the job you wanted? The bills are piling up? Remember that your reaction to each situation—whether weak or strong—is the only thing that can hurt you, so choose it well. We can choose to cower in the face of life's failures, or we can hand our pain over to God, receive from His grace, and take your next breath of faith.

Mandy's been admitted to the hospital more than one hundred times, not counting visits for research, blood work, or doctor's appointments. Yet somehow the Young family has managed to say that happiness leads to health, and without it we can't live life to its fullest. In the face of adversity, all they could do is find a way to laugh and to bring joy to others through laughter as well. It's a big thing in their lives to embrace humor, and I've seen that at forty thousand feet in the air.

The Pantry
CHOCKED-FULL OF FOOD FOR THOUGHT

The Main Ingredient

Contentment is hard to come by sometimes, especially when it feels like the world is against us. But we can take steps to move ourselves toward a contented life. We can count our blessings for one. Just by looking around us, we can see the many wonderful things that God is doing in our life, but we need to be willing to look. Accept who you are and give thanks that you're one of a kind.

A Slice of Advice

Dear Candace,

A friend of mine told me that she took her daughter to see you when you were in Columbus, Ohio, and they absolutely loved your testimony. I'm crazy jealous now because I was your biggest fan growing up, and I probably still am. I watched every episode of Full House *and now my daughter and I are watching* Make It or Break It *together. We're both excited that you have a Christian testimony.*

I live in Odessa, Texas, and I was wondering if you ever travel out here to speak? My daughter and I would love to meet you and get an autographed photo if possible.

—Stephanie

Dear Stephanie,

It's exciting to know that I have a mother and daughter team cheering me on in Texas!

I travel to churches around the U.S. so often that I'm bound to get out to your area one of these days. And now I hope that I will! If you're not following me on Twitter, I suggest that you do because the readers there are always updated on what's happening next. So if I'm going to be in your area, you'll probably see me tweeting about it.

Also check out my Web site at www.candacecameronbure.net, where you'll find a calendar announcing my upcoming speaking engagements. I always post them months in advance.

If you don't want to wait, you can purchase personally autographed photos, copies of my testimony on CD, and T-shirts. Just go to the shop link.

Keep watching Make It or Break It, *and I hope to see you both soon!*
—Candace

A Pinch of Practicality

If you are looking for ways to burn extra calories or get in a little exercise, here are a few practical steps you can take:

- Park far away in a parking lot. Why look for a close spot when you can seize the opportunity to get a few extra steps in?
- Always try to take the stairs. I always do. Even if it's ten floors. In the mall, take the stairs.
- Walk wherever you can. We live in a place where there are coffee shops and restaurants within a mile or two. Instead of taking the car, we often walk.
- Shovel the snow or mow the lawn before your husband comes home. A lot of women wait for the man to do the job, but it's an awesome opportunity to exercise and surprise your husband in the process.

You'll find cities where people are thinner in general. Cities like New York, Toronto, and European cities in general because they are walking cities.

People spend too much time in their car these days, so change that and make a point of walking where you can. If you have groceries to pick up or you have to go to the post office, walking there will benefit you with fresh air and exercise.

The Candy Dish

Contentment is a pearl of great price, and whoever procures it at the expense of ten thousand desires makes a wise and a happy purchase. —John Balguy

From My Stove to Yours

Turkey Meatloaf

INGREDIENTS

1 lb of ground turkey
1 egg
½ cup of Italian style bread crumbs
½ cup Old Fashioned Quaker Oats
2 cloves garlic, minced
1 small onion, chopped
½ cup ketchup
¼ cup mustard

DIRECTIONS

Combine all ingredients. You'll have to roll up your sleeves and mix this one by hand. Press into a meatloaf or bread pan and cook at 350 degrees for 45 minutes or until cooked through.

FOURTEEN

Learn the Art of Dining Out

Each and every time I close my front door, I leave with the knowledge that health is a twenty-four-hour commitment. I know I'll be busy, I know I'll be on the road, and I know that time could work against me at any moment. But with that knowledge I also know that regardless of what comes my way, I have options to choose from that work for the health of my body. I share this mind-set with Val and the kids. It's important to all of us that we live well, whether at home or at work. Health is one thing Val and I both have in common, and we strive to instill it in the lives of our kids.

I love food. I love the smell, I love the taste, I love the variety. But I think we all have to come to terms with the fact that first and foremost, food is fuel for our bodies. Let's get the entertainment aspect of it out of our heads for a minute and realize that it doesn't have to be a 24-7 buffet.

God calls us to be content, and contentment cannot abide with greed, nor can it abide with self-pity. A content person will be just as happy to eat an entree in a restaurant as she will a salad on the go. I've learned to appreciate abundance, and I've learned also to appreciate those times when I've had to skip a meal or grab a granola bar as I'm heading out the door.

> *For I have learned to be content whatever the circumstances. I know what it is to be in need, and I know what it is to have plenty. I have learned the secret of being content in any and every situation, whether well fed or hungry, whether living in plenty or in want. (Phil. 4:11–12)*

Val and I both love good food. When dining out, we'll check out the top-rated and best new restaurants to see what the buzz is all about. It's great to go to a new restaurant on date night. I'll call a babysitter so we can have some adult time, and off we'll go dressed in our LA best.

The restaurants can be pricey, but the food looks as beautiful on the plate as it is delicious. We love to pair food and wine. In fact, since retiring from hockey, Val launched his own wine label in 2007 out of Napa Valley, California, "Bure Family Wines."

We like to experiment and don't hesitate when ordering food we've never tasted before. In fact, we like to try as many new items as we possibly can. It's not uncommon for each of us to order an appetizer or two apiece as well as an entree, and regardless of what we order, we trade halfway through our meal. However, just because I have a lot of food on my plate, that doesn't mean I eat it all. I'll have four or five bites of each thing and put it off to the side. My taste buds experience a full palette of flavor when I'm eating out. For Val and me fine dining is something we splurge on. Some spend on jewelry, others spend on cars, and we like to spend on fine food. And I've gotten over the issue of bringing home a doggy bag. Restaurants serve portions way too big, and I order way too much. In most cases I wouldn't hesitate to ask.

Going to a restaurant can be a treat, but for that reason we often feel entitled to go for it and eat whatever we want regardless of whether or not it's a good choice. Sometimes there might be so many options that our eyes start to wander into the land of decadence. Instead of focusing on what you shouldn't be eating, think of all the wonderfully healthy choices on the menu that you don't have to cook! Dining out shouldn't be an excuse for so-called deserved indulgence, so if you have so many good things to choose from, why would you need to indulge?

Here's where contentment comes into play. Ask yourself what's best for your body, and stick with that plan. If you've already eaten a large lunch, then maybe you'll want to have an appetizer-size portion for dinner. Or if you've had a bagel for breakfast and pasta for lunch—two high-carb meals—you might want to go for a salad with some protein or a vegetable dish for your dinner. Don't grumble or dwell on a feeling of discontentment because you're not getting all that you hoped for. Instead stop hoping and be content with what you have.

When I'm out to dinner, I won't even glance at the pasta section on the menu. I just don't look. I don't tempt myself by reading the write-up and considering the option. I don't say, "I really, really want this cream sauce with bacon, but, ugh, I have to eat a salad!" (frown). I don't eat pasta at night, and I'm aware of those boundaries because I determined them beforehand. I can go through my head, recap what I ate for breakfast and lunch, and then make the best choice for dinner. I won't salivate over something I don't want to consider.

A devout life does bring wealth, but it's the rich simplicity of being yourself before God. Since we entered the world penniless and will leave it penniless, if we have bread on the table and shoes on our feet, that's enough. (1 Tim. 6:6–8 The Message)

When I speak at church events, they often take me to restaurants, but sometimes they have big potlucks. I've gotta tell you that some of that southern food sure does surprise me! Don't get me wrong, it tastes great, but heavy butter, mayo, deep-dish casseroles, fried everything, and melted cheese . . . I could run screaming to the nearest deli, or I could take direction from God who wants me to be content with the food that I have.

In those situations I'm really just thankful that I have been given a meal at all, and I make do. I'll take small portions of cream spinach, lasagna, macaroni casserole, and pasta salads. Although I am really happy if I find a piece of lettuce or tomato in there somewhere!

Bottom line is that if someone has gone to an effort for you, such as dinner at a friend's house, or delivered a meal when you're sick, make an exception to your rule and accept the food with thanks. Make the best choices you can within the parameters offered to you, and don't always expect to pamper your palette.

By now you know I don't eat fast food. Burgers, fries, pizza, etc., are not foods I typically eat. If I'm working, I know I'll need energy, so I choose food that will give me fuel. Bread and cheese will weigh me down. I need protein and vegetables for energy and stamina, especially when I'm sharing my testimony to an audience of thousands. I know I'll be on my feet all night speaking, meeting and greeting many people after the event.

I always travel with a companion, so I'm rarely alone. Sometimes we are short on time when I arrive at a city and don't always have time to sit down and eat. If that's the case, I will ask if there is a sandwich shop or a place like Panera Bread nearby where we can grab a quick salad. If my only option is a typical fast food joint, I'll pass. I won't starve. I can wait. It's a brilliant opportunity just to skip it and donate to a charity close to my heart, http://www.skip1.org. I skip a meal, and they feed a child! Now my hunger pains are really doing some good. Skipping a meal is always an option for me when I have limited choices.

Because of traveling and work, I've dined out a lot over the years. In fact, when I was young, the majority of my meals were at restaurants. There were certain years, when I was on *Full House* and my brother Kirk was on *Growing Pains* that our busy schedules were so much for our parents it was crazy. At that time we ate out a lot more than we did at home, but that didn't mean that I was allowed to eat French fries and drink milk shakes all night. My parents still ensured that we ordered a reasonably healthy meal, whether we wanted to or not.

I eat at home more now than I ever did, and I love it because Val's a great chef. The kids have school and sports, and we have our routine, so we'll eat at home during the week. But on Friday nights we like to take them out too. My kids know how to behave and enjoy dinner at a nice restaurant. I love that Maks likes putting on his "nice" jeans and fancy button-down shirt. He sprays on some of Val's cologne and makes sure his hair looks nice. That being said, long dinners aren't always their favorite thing to do. They prefer something quicker, which might be a Mexican restaurant like Chipotle, La Salsa, or Baja Fresh, but regardless of where we go, Val and I ensure that they make wise choices when they order. Kids like to complain. I know that as much as any mom. But the more I have taught them to try new food and make nutritious choices, the more they have come to like it. With a bit of practice and a good attitude, contentment is something we can all train ourselves to accept.

Health isn't just about the food we eat or how much exercise we get in a day; it's also about attitude. Approaching weight loss with a sense of contentment will bring you a lot further than a sense of entitlement ever will. Suppressing our desires can be hard at times, but if we go at it with a good attitude, we start to see that our half-empty glass is half full. Attitude powers motivation, and motivation is exactly what we need to move on.

I'm reminded of a Bible verse that talks about fasting. I think it's also a really good lesson to apply to our diet.

> *When you fast, do not look somber as the hypocrites do,*
> *for they disfigure their faces to show men they are fasting.*
> *I tell you the truth, they have received their reward in full.*
> *(Matt. 6:16)*

We entertain a lot, usually on the weekend. We'll fire up the barbeque, make a few salads, and have family and friends over. If I'm cutting back on my meal, or if I happen to be fasting that day (for prayer purposes, never to lose weight), I don't feel the need to announce, "Hey, I'm dying for a piece of that salmon." Or, "Man, I wish this fast was over already!" I know and the Lord knows what's going on, and that's good enough for me.

I just grab a glass of water and join in the conversation as I normally would. No one really notices, and everyone has a good time. At the end of the day, I'm not any worse off. The grilled salmon will still be there tomorrow, and I can always eat then.

I'm blessed when it comes to lunch at work because I have a lot of choices. A catering truck comes to the studio lot and provides breakfast and lunch at specified times. There is always a buffet with hot food including different types of vegetables, rice, pasta, and meat. Some days they might grill chicken breasts, beef burgers, or crab cakes. Other times they have a pasta bar with grilled shrimp, sausages, and other toppings. It changes daily, and I'll often just eat there since it's easy and free. I can sit in my dressing room, eat my lunch, and relax.

I know we are called to be content with what we're given, but I also know that there's a flip side to that when wisdom and boundaries need to kick in. I once did a movie called *No One Would Tell*. An assistant on set was so sweet to me that she kept preparing a tray of food from the craft service table and putting it in my room every morning. I would walk in there each day and find doughnuts, muffins, cookies, and soda pop, which is all horribly fattening and sugary food. I didn't want to throw them out, but I didn't want to eat it either.

I finally had to come out and say, "Thank you so much for thinking of me, but I really don't want to eat this type of food, especially since I avoid the snack table."

That was fifteen years ago, right before I got married. People still watch that movie, and they are still showing it in schools. As for me, I'm still avoiding the snack table, and I can still fit into my wedding dress!

All this to say that regardless of where you are or what you are given, you have the option to make good choices for your health. I have eaten everywhere including church basements, airplanes, fast-food joints, and fine dining establishments, and in each case I do my best to honor my body by giving it the best option I can. I encourage you to do the same. If you're concerned about an upcoming night out because you know that you'll be eating in a restaurant, seize the opportunity to make a good choice for a change—without complaint. If you can stop looking at dining out as an entitlement to pamper your passion, you'll discover a new way of living that doesn't stop when you leave your front door.

The Pantry
CHOCKED-FULL OF FOOD FOR THOUGHT

The Main Ingredient

Eating well shouldn't stop when you leave the house. In fact restaurants offer us the perfect opportunity to make a good choice. We are so used to pampering our passion instead of looking at food as fuel that we make the wrong choice time and again. If we start training ourselves to be content with the food we require, whether that food is a salad or a steak, we begin to grow into healthy, mature eaters.

A Slice of Advice

Dear Candace,

I remember watching you on Full House and learning so much from each episode as a kid. Not only have you been a role model, but there have been so many things that you went through on the show that I've been through in real life. At one point I even had a struggle with eating and thinking the same things that DJ did. Recently I found out that you were a Christian, and your testimony just really touched my heart.

I am in college and hoping to get into the entertainment industry for set design. At the same time I'm so afraid that I will not be able to stand my ground in what I believe and do what I need both career-wise and spiritually. Can you give me some tips that have helped keep you firm and strong in your career?

God bless,

—Leslie

Dear Leslie,

I hope school is going well for you. I loved your question: how can you stand firm in your faith while working in the entertainment industry?

It's simple. There's no difference between the entertainment industry and any other job you might have! You'll always run into people who don't share the same point of view, who don't believe in God, who believe in other gods, and who will think you're silly for loving Jesus. I realized when I went back to work that no matter where you are, what career you have, whether you're a student or a mom of five, that as a Christian you have a wonderful opportunity to be a light in this world to others. Simply do your job well with a joyful heart, doing your work for the Lord. Be kind to your coworkers and boss so that they see a difference in you and want to know what it is. That's part of what being a Christian is all about. Take the time to share your faith with others, and if they aren't open to the discussion, allow Jesus to shine through you in your efforts at work.

My new show isn't a "Christian" show, but it doesn't mean I'm not doing the work and will of my Father every day I'm there.

My tips are to start your day off in prayer, inviting the Holy Spirit in each morning and putting on the armor of God as found in Ephesians 6:10–18.

—Candace

A Pinch of Practicality

If you've lost weight or you want to maintain, make sure your clothing fits well, and alter any clothing that doesn't. Don't hang on to large sizes because it only gives you an excuse to put the lost weight back on. It's one thing to have a few comfy sweatpants for days you feel bloated, but don't keep a pair of oversized jeans.

If you dropped a few sizes, there isn't any reason the size twelves should still be hanging around unless you expect to return to that size. Clean out the old clothes and believe that this change is for good. Give them to your favorite charity, or send them off to a friend, but get them out of your sight.

If the big clothes are gone and your pants start to fill snug, you won't have anything to fall back on. The only choice you'll have is to buckle down on bad habits again.

Maintaining is a lot easier than letting ten pounds creep up and having to go at it all over again.

Food for Thought

A recap of Scripture to meditate on:

- For I have learned to be content whatever the circumstances. I know what it is to be in need, and I know what it is to have plenty. I have learned the secret of being content in any and every situation, whether well fed or hungry, whether living in plenty or in want. (Phil. 4:11–12)
- A devout life does bring wealth, but it's the rich simplicity of being yourself before God. Since we entered the world penniless and will leave it penniless, if we have bread on the table and shoes on our feet, that's enough. (1 Tim. 6:6–8 *The Message*)
- When you fast, do not look somber as the hypocrites do, for they disfigure their faces to show men they are fasting. I tell you the truth, they have received their reward in full. (Matt. 6:16)

The Candy Dish

Restaurants with peppermills the size of fire extinguishers and big red menus with the entries spelled with F's instead of S's are always expensive. —Miss Piggy, Miss Piggy's Guide to Life

From My Stove to Yours

French Toast

Serves 4

INGREDIENTS

> 4 large eggs
> ¼ cup crushed pineapple
> 4 to 6 slices of cinnamon raisin bread (or whole wheat)
> ¼ teaspoon cinnamon
> Cooking spray
> Cottage cheese or berry jam

DIRECTIONS

Whisk the eggs and stir in pineapple and cinnamon. Add the bread slices and turn them in the mixture to soak for about thirty seconds per side.

Coat a nonstick skillet with cooking spray and set over medium to high heat.

Once the pan is hot, add the bread slices and cook until golden brown (about two to three minutes per side).

Serve warm with syrup or cottage cheese and berry jam.

FIFTEEN

A House Swept Clean

It had been several years since the bad habits were put to rest. I was making good choices, controlling my portions, and attending to the needs of my health.

Finally my spiritual life was right on track. I was getting stronger as a Christian, and together as a family we were learning about the Lord. We had moved to the east coast, where Val was playing hockey with the Florida Panthers, and we had settled in to a place we called home. Val had started attending church with us, and I was digging into the Word. I was studying the Bible, learning who God is, and listening to His voice in my life. Things were going strong for me spiritually.

But for whatever reason unknown to me at the time, I was back in a desert of testing. The lure of the pantry was calling my name while Val was on the road, and I returned to the food to find comfort. I found myself stuffed, and with that stuffed feeling also came the feeling of shame. I had done so well for so many years, and again I was gripped by an appetite that was ruling my head.

The cycle of sneaking late-night snacks was back and consumed my thoughts in a matter of days. I knew it wasn't good for my body, but passion trumped wisdom time and again. After a while it didn't matter if I was filling some sort of a void or not, I just found comfort in food. I didn't really want Val to know I had fallen off track so I'd usually pull out the snacks when he wasn't around.

There was no logical reason I did it, other than the fact that it had a grip on me. Why was this returning? And why was it worse than it had been for years?

> When an evil spirit comes out of a man, it goes through arid places seeking rest and does not find it. Then it says, "I will return to the house I left." When it arrives, it finds the house unoccupied, swept clean and put in order. Then it goes and takes with it seven other spirits more wicked than itself, and they go in and live there. And the final condition of that man is worse than the first. That is how it will be with this wicked generation. (Matt. 12:43–45)

The above parable illustrates the difference between a moral reformation and a spiritual transformation. I had been living a moral life for as long as I could remember. I had put my bad habits away. But it wasn't until I realized my behavior was nothing less than sin that I finally saw gluttony in its true light. My house was swept clean and put in order, bad habits were put away, but a spiritual battle was yet to be won.

God was requiring more of me. Being good wasn't good enough. If I was to really be transformed by the Spirit as I was seeking to be, He wanted every area of my life to be handled in a *spiritual* way.

I was learning the important lesson that morality is weak, but the Spirit is strong.

I was struggling with something that I couldn't manage on my own. I didn't feel right, but regardless of that I continued to do it. I didn't want to do it; I had to do it. I hated being that person I saw in the mirror. Sneaking around, losing control, gaining what I thought was control. . . . Sound familiar?

> *I do not understand what I do. For what I want to do I do
> not do, but what I hate I do. (Rom. 7:15)*

Satan clearly knew my weakness, and God allowed Him to explore that weakness and tempt me with it. I was a mess, hiding snacks and sneaking sweets late at night. Here I was striving to learn about God, loving my new relationship with Him, and my passion was in a battle for control of my spirit. Ice cream was in supply, and I was in bondage to food.

I wanted to get back on track. I saw how great Val was with self-control, and I couldn't understand why I was faced with a struggle that came so easy to him. I hadn't talked in great detail with him about it. Being that he was an athlete, I didn't know if he could really understand. He excelled in self-discipline, and I lacked self-control.

It came to a halt one Sunday when Val was on the road playing a hockey game, and I was at church with the kids. They were in Sunday school while I listened to our pastor speak. I don't recall what the sermon was about, but I do remember that by the end of it, I had started to cry—hard. It was the kind of sermon that grabbed hold of my heart, and I knew it was time to listen. God was speaking to me. I couldn't help myself, but He was willing and able to help.

Minutes later I was standing in front of our pastor with tears streaming down my face.

"Candace, what's the matter? Do you want to talk?" he asked.

"Yes I do," I replied, "I need help."

I felt that this stronghold was hindering my growth. I didn't know why it was happening or where it had come from, but I knew I couldn't find freedom on my own.

We talked, and I listened while he explained. What I was doing was physical, yes, but my spiritual battle needed to be handled in a spiritual way. I was a blossoming Christian bringing our family to church. Five people in my house were learning to serve the Lord, and Satan wasn't about to let that pass without a struggle.

"Now that you're walking in faith," he said, "Satan is using your weakness to discourage you—to pull you away and destroy your testimony."

I did feel discouraged. I had been doing so well for so long, but somehow I had gotten off track. Getting off track seemed easy, but getting back on was a war I couldn't win on my own.

Our pastor suggested I talk to a friend of theirs who had once battled the same struggle. Stacy and I had lunch, compared stories, and shared our faith. It felt great to talk to someone who went through it too and had conquered it with Jesus.

"Candace, I know in your heart you love the Lord," she said, "but do you know that what you are doing is sin?"

Her words gave me a new perspective on things. I had always viewed my appetite and the struggles it caused as being a moral issue, having never understood the spiritual battle I faced. What I was doing was sin. My house was swept clean, but there was still plenty of dirt hiding under the rug. Now that I was living and walk-ing in the Spirit, God knew that weakness was still present. He knew that the battle had not been won. Satan took that opportunity to sift me like wheat, and God allowed it so that the victory would be His.

I knew that abusing my body with food was a bad habit for me, but since I wasn't hurting anyone else, I hadn't seen it as sin. I finally understood. He created me. My body is a temple to be used by Him and for Him. He desires that we seek a *spiritual* transformation, not merely a *moral* one.

That talk hit me as nothing before had done. I wanted nothing to do with sin that is willfully and knowingly wrong. That was it.

The urge remained for a while, but I refused to sin against God. Instead I would pray, "I love you, God. Help me to walk away from food. Through You I have freedom of choice." I walked through many weeks both believing and saying that prayer.

To this day I don't struggle with food as I once did. But if the thought ever popped into my head, I know that there isn't anything Jesus Himself hasn't been tempted with and yet remained sinless. God won't give me more than I can handle and always provides a way for escape. I choose that escape when I walk away from the fridge. I have a choice: I can open a tub of ice cream, or I can walk into another room and read a book. I have choices, and I keep it in check by making the right ones. I want to please God, I want Him to be happy with me, and I want to be a good servant to Him. That is my goal.

After I talked with my pastor and met with Stacy, I wanted to share my struggles with Val. I felt vulnerable. Would he get it? Would he understand how much I lacked self-control and how difficult this journey might be for me?

His father, who smoked for years, went to his doctor who said, "Quit smoking, or you may have a heart attack." That was it—no patch, no weaning, no nothing. He quit. It was as simple as that.

Val has that same level of self-control. For him self-control seems to come easy, and I was concerned he might expect that level from me. I explained to him what a struggle this was in my life. He didn't have the response I was expecting at all. Instead he listened to my struggle with sympathy, he was happy I shared it with him, and I was happy too. He said he would pray with me and help me along the way.

I felt disgusted, unhealthy, and out of control, but now I wonder if perhaps God allowed me to walk through this fire so I'd be equipped to comfort those who walk through it too. I can say that I know what you're going through if you are gripped by food. I am finally free, and you can be too.

Don't be surprised if you fall off the wagon. Many of us on the health train find it's going well for a while, but then as we're digging deeper into the Word, we face a relapse. Be prepared. The enemy is trying to knock us off course. There may be a point where you trip up, fall on your face, and return to bad habits. I've been there. I've done that. Through Christ we can dust ourselves off and get back in the race. Even when we don't believe in ourselves, Jesus believes in us enough to put out His hand and pull us back on the track.

Many women who have lost weight gain it all back and then some. Of course they ask themselves, "Why bother if I just repeat the same cycle?"

I say because it's different when you're fighting the battle with Christ on your side. Keep a healthy body for Him, and you won't fail the same way as you did in the past.

I'm healthy because I want to be used by God to the best of my ability and as much as He'll allow me to be used. Health, fitness, and size act to glorify Him in my line of work. In my industry I need to stay in shape and be fit so I can get the types of roles I like and with those roles glorify Him. By doing that, I become a living testimony.

The entertainment industry is largely based on vanity. There is a standard I need to keep with each project I do. My goal is not to have an amazing body when I hit the next magazine cover (although that'd be nice!). It's that in everything I do, including my work, I want to glorify the Lord.

Weight loss and health are specific to each one of us; therefore we shouldn't be looking beside us for that measuring stick of self-control, size, or beauty. I can't compare myself to Val any more than you should compare yourself to other women at the gym. We're uniquely created, each facing our own set of circumstances and struggles.

If you're being tested, I'll tell you why. God is requiring more of you. Being good isn't good enough. If you really want to be transformed by the Spirit, as I hope you are seeking to be, He wants every area of your life to be handled in a *spiritual* way.

The Pantry
CHOCKED-FULL OF FOOD FOR THOUGHT

The Main Ingredient

When dealing with bad habits we have, we need to ask ourselves if we are battling a moral or a spiritual issue. If what we are doing is hurting our walk with the Lord, then we need to come to a place of true repentance where we are down on our knees before the Lord asking for forgiveness and help.

A Slice of Advice

Dear Candace,

First off, I just want to say what a true blessing you are to me! So thank you so much for your time and great words!

Lately it seems that I have a hard time letting go of the sins I have committed in the past. I know I have been forgiven due to asking God for forgiveness and basically saying that I am sorry, but I still think about things I have done, and it brings me to tears sometimes.

I rededicated my life to God a few months back. I have been visiting churches in my area, but it's been hard, trying to back away from "worldly" things that are out there.

I was brought up in a Christian home. My grandfather is a preacher at the church I went to in my hometown, and at age twelve I was saved by asking God to come into my heart and forgive me as a sinner. When I graduated from high school and started college, I started going down the wrong path, and then I would feel guilty and ask for forgiveness. Only a few months ago I realized I needed to change and start putting God first in everything I do. I know that if we ask God to forgive us, we are forgiven, but how do I shake this feeling of "why did I do that?"

I have been reading my Bible, and I just got the book you recommended: The Way of the Master. Any advice you have would be great!
—Renee

Dear Renee,

Thanks for your e-mail. I'm so glad you got The Way of the Master because that's the book I'd recommend reading.

I suspect you've never come to a place of godly sorrow. I'm talking in tears, on your knees, over the sin in your life. It's a place so deep inside of you, where you understand how offensive you've been toward God. Then understanding what He did for you on the cross and His grace.

I know you know "all the words" and what they mean, but I don't know that you've been affected by it in your soul. It didn't happen for me until after I read The Way of the Master. Maybe this will trigger it for you too, or maybe it will be something else.

In any case, once you've experienced godly sorrow, you can come to a place of true repentance. Asking God to forgive you, and turning *from your sin. See, it's not just about feeling guilty over it and confessing it but feeling so sorrowful that you don't want to do it anymore. When you've asked for that forgiveness, it's been given to you. There's no reason to wallow in the guilt; that's not going to do anything. You have to trust that once you're forgiven, you're forgiven.*

"Therefore, my brothers, I want you to know that through Jesus the forgiveness of sins is proclaimed to you (Acts 13:38). Move on, and move into a right relationship with God. Dig into the Word to get to know Him better and what He wants to do with your life.

—Candace

A Pinch of Practicality

Stop beating yourself up over the mistakes you've made, and start rewarding yourself for the good choices your make. One way to do this is by keeping a jar close by into which you drop a coin each time you make a conscious effort that benefits your body, soul, or spirit.

You'll discover that the little choices we make add up quickly. Decide to use the money at the end of each month to reward yourself in some way. With the money you've saved, buy a pair of earrings, a lip gloss, or (if you've saved enough) a great pair of jeans. It will make you feel good and encourage you to make wise decisions more often.

Food For Thought

- When an evil spirit comes out of a man, it goes through arid places seeking rest and does not find it. Then it says, "I will return to the house I left." When it arrives, it finds the house unoccupied, swept clean and put in order. Then it goes and takes with it seven other spirits more wicked than itself, and they go in and live there. And the final condition of that man is worse than the first. That is how it will be with this wicked generation. (Matt. 12:43–45)

- I do not understand what I do. For what I want to do I do not do, but what I hate I do. (Rom. 7:15)

The Candy Dish

Great effort is required to arrest decay and restore vigor. One must exercise proper deliberation, plan carefully before making a move, and be alert in guarding against relapse following a renaissance. —Horace, Roman poet

From My Stove to Yours

Lemon and Dill Baked Salmon

Serves 4

INGREDIENTS

8 thin slices fresh lemon
4 (6 to 8-ounce) skinless salmon fillets
Sea salt and freshly ground black pepper
2 tablespoons of freshly chopped dill
1 tablespoon olive oil

DIRECTIONS

Preheat the oven to 375 degrees.

Season each salmon fillet with salt and pepper and place in a large 9 x 13 shallow baking dish. Lay two lemon slices on top of each fillet. Mix oil and dill and pour over the salmon. Bake for 10 to 15 minutes.

SIXTEEN

It Is Well with My Soul

I'll never forget that morning—how cold the air felt around me, while the warmth of God's hand waxed my soul. We went in for the pre-op appointment and met with the surgeon. It was the first time he was able to look at the CT scans and provide us with an informed analysis. In our previous meetings, he went off the reports, but that morning, after closely reviewing the films, he was able to give us the full diagnosis. It wasn't good. We were looking at a *cholesteatoma*, which is a cystic mass, or an accumulation of dead cells, much like a tumor, in the middle ear. Unfortunately the cholesteatoma was not in the early stages and had in fact been there for a while. It was quite large. If left untreated, the mass would cause permanent deafness and move on to other areas of the body, including the brain.

He then told us that they would have to do a much more invasive procedure that would involve not only removing the cholesteatoma but also cutting out much of the cartilage, causing a wide-open hole in our little boy's ear that would be prone to serious infection. If this was to be done, Lev would never be able to get his ear wet or swim again for the rest of his life. At four years old Lev was already a master diver, and so the thought of separating him from the water he loved so much was heartbreaking for us.

The doctor also warned us three times saying, "Be prepared for the possibility of facial nerve damage because the size of the cholesteatoma has severely wrapped itself around those nerves."

It was an emotionally exhausting day, preparing for the worst yet hoping for the best. I would have loved to have heard better news, but his words didn't fall in our favor.

Lev is my saving grace. He's tenderhearted, sensitive, and truly has a heart for God. Some say he's the spitting image of me with his little round nose and almond-shaped eyes. Regardless of how much effort I do or don't put into growing his faith, he loves the Lord. He's diligent in all that he does, whether it's getting his homework done or his chores. Bright and intelligent, he is a straight-A student, and his teachers never cease to tell me what a joy he is to teach. Like his dad, he's a genetically gifted athlete, competing in tennis and hockey, and playing just about any sport you could possibly imagine. I love his smile.

That smile was present the morning we arrived at the hospital. In spite of his condition, his courage shone through, offering a sense of peace to both Val and me. We arrived at 6:30 a.m., he was in surgery by 11:20 a.m., and for the next hour we prayed, patiently waiting for news.

Words can't describe the joy that flooded our hearts the moment the nurse spoke those words, "They are performing the lesser of two surgeries." And while we waited another hour or so for the doctor to give us the final news, we knew the grace of God was upon us and that Lev would indeed be okay.

The surgery went well. The cholesteatoma was large indeed, but they kept working at it and were able to remove it without opening the inner ear canal. There wasn't any facial nerve damage whatsoever, but out of the three hearing bones, two of them had already been destroyed. They removed those two as well as half of the remaining bone. His little head was wrapped in bandages, and while his body was weak, his spirit was strong. Lev is nearly deaf in his right ear, which is truly the least of our worries.

It was an exhausting experience for any parent to go through, but we found comfort in knowing that so many people were praying over Lev and the doctors, and for that we are eternally grateful. Faith and prayer carried us through, along with a sense of peace and assurance that only comes from the Lord, the greatest physician of all.

> "Do not be anxious about anything, but in everything, by prayer and petition, with thanksgiving, present your requests to God. And the peace of God, which transcends all understanding, will guard your hearts and your minds in Christ Jesus." (Phil. 4:6–7)

The peace of God has been a lifeline for me over the years. When I'm tired, stressed out, angry, or at the end of my rope, I try my best to remember, "It is well with my soul." I know that regardless of what I am put through on Earth, my spirit cannot be touched, I can rest in that knowledge because I am safe in His arms. He is my shield.

Say the word *affliction*, and you can't help remembering the Israelites. They finally fled Egypt, leaving a life of slavery behind them; and before they knew it, Pharaoh was hot on their tail. God hardened the heart of Pharaoh knowing that he would pursue them and as a result was able to show His power to save.

Imagine it this way: say you make a decision to live well today. You decide that you're going to start eating well, and you plan to walk thirty minutes every day, starting tomorrow! You've decided that you've lived in bondage to food far too long, and you want to leave it behind in search of the promised land. A land flowing with milk and honey, where you are free from the pull of the fridge door, and you are in the groove of a fitness routine.

So you wake up in the morning, ready to take on the world; but before you do, things start to fall out of place. Nothing works out as you planned. Stress is on the rise. And as the problems begin to accumulate, your day is thrown into a spin and your plans along with it.

That's when you just might decide in your heart, "I didn't expect to deal with all of this right now—it's too much. I'm tired, I'm stressed, and all I can think of is sinking my teeth into the nearest loaf of French bread and zoning out on the couch. I'm better off returning to the life I had. After all, it was never really that bad."

This thought has been echoed throughout the ages, starting way back as far as Exodus 14:11–12 when the Israelites asked, "What have you done to us by bringing us out of Egypt? Didn't we say to you in Egypt, 'Leave us alone; let us serve the Egyptians'? It would have been better for us to serve the Egyptians than to die in the desert!"

When you are standing in the desert of testing with your back to the sea and all you can see in front of you is the enemy closing in, be still. Stand firm, and you will find deliverance. Have you ever stood still long enough to witness God do His work? Have you ever stood still in His presence and let Him fight your enemy? Be still. Because when you do, God will triumph over your enemy, release you from your stronghold, and you will know that He is God.

God hardened Pharaoh's heart so he would pursue the Israelites, but when he did, God not only rescued His people, but He also sabotaged the pursuit of the Egyptians by removing their chariot wheels and finally covering them with the sea. Can you hear the sound of the Israelites rejoicing at the sight? Can you hear the sound of your own voice rejoicing when you press on in faith and let God destroy the enemy that you leave behind?

I absolutely love reading the stories from the Old Testament because there is so much to glean from them. The events they lived through typify my walk with Christ in so many ways. *So many.* Whether they are about slavery in Egypt, the time spent in the wilderness, crossing the Red Sea, or entering the promised land. Those stories teach us lessons that we can apply to our lives today. Each lesson shows the power of God, so that we might have hope for today.

Hope. Did you read that? That we might have hope! There is a desert of testing. I won't deny that or sugarcoat it in any way. It will be hard before it gets easy. In fact, it is often God's style to wait until the storm is at its fullest before He commands the waves to cease. That's how we learn to lean on Him. If it was easy, we'd all be model thin and run three miles a day. Life isn't easy, but that's okay. Let that thought sink in for a minute: Life isn't easy, but that's okay. In fact it's better than okay, when we consider the maturity it brings to our souls.

> *"Consider it pure joy, my brothers, whenever you face trials of many kinds, because you know that the testing of your faith develops perseverance. Perseverance must finish its work so that you may be mature and complete, not lacking anything." (James 1:2–4)*

God desires to triumph over our enemies. He desires to rescue you from your stronghold. He desires to lead you to the promised land. Will you let Him?

Perseverance takes patience, a characteristic that most of us lack. Two weeks at a gym and women are discouraged that the weight isn't coming off yet. Even a slow computer can get us in a tailspin. Life takes time, and we need to remember that—it takes time.

If you give up and return to Egypt at the first sign of trouble, you're missing out on blessings God has to offer. You're missing out on the promise He gives to trample our enemies under His feet.

What happens at the second sign of trouble—if you plateau for a week, two weeks, or a month? If it rains just as you plan to go out for a walk—every time? Will you, like the Israelites, grumble once again, longing for the day when you ate all of the bread you wanted? That's what they did. Even after crossing the Red Sea, a miracle we can barely imagine, let alone feel beneath our feet. They wanted to return to slavery because they were hungry and too impatient to wait on God for their food. Not unlike us.

C. S. Lewis wrote, "A silly idea is current that good people do not know what temptation means. This is an obvious lie. Only those who try to resist temptation know how strong it is. . . . A man who gives in to temptation after five minutes simply does not know what it would have been like an hour later. That is why bad people, in one sense, know very little about badness. They have lived a sheltered life by always giving in."[3]

He speaks to the weakness many of us face from time to time. We become the five-minute girl, giving into temptation left, right, and center. Perhaps it's lack of sleep, which is a popular reason we hang off the wagon while our feet drag on the ground, or it might be a case of stress. Whatever the reason, we return to the food thinking, *Tomorrow will be a better day.* And we believe that it will.

If I have learned anything from my experience with trials, it's this: I need to take that step of patience now—not tonight, not tomorrow—right now. Push the food to the side today. Why? Because it's not going to comfort me the way that I think it will. And guess what? That food will still be there tomorrow.

Some might say, "It's just food. Get real!" But no, it's not just food any more than gold is just gold. When your life molds or shapes it into something you idolize, or use to tranquilize, it becomes your golden calf.

I could have returned to the food when Lev was in the hospital. Those hours in the waiting room I could have been spent filling my face, but instead I chose to fast, pray, and fill my heart with the knowledge that God was fighting this battle and that He was in control.

How it must pain God when He frees us from slavery, whether it be to food, alcohol, overspending, smoking, binging, purging . . . whatever our stronghold is, only to find us returning to it once again, hoping to find tranquility—excusing the struggle we have with our weakness so we can worship and cling to the calf once again.

God doesn't always provide the easy way out. He doesn't promise that life will be a breeze or free of temptation; in fact temptation is something we can always expect. But what He does promise us is this: He'll always provide a way to escape. There's always a way out—a better way to escape from our pain—and with a little soul searching and determination, a way to leave the gold calf behind.

These things happened to them as examples and were written down as warnings for us, on whom the fulfillment of the ages has come. So, if you think you are standing firm, be careful that you don't fall! No temptation has seized you except what is common to man. And God is faithful; he will not let you be tempted beyond what you can bear. But when you are

*tempted, he will also provide a way out so that you can stand
up under it. (1 Cor. 10:11–13)*

Whenever I've been tempted to run to the bathroom after eating
too much, this verse instantly comes to mind. When faced with the
truth, knowing that I have another choice because God promised
me so, do I take God's hand? Or do I turn my back on Him and dive
into my sin? I know my decision. What about you?

The Pantry

CHOCKED-FULL OF FOOD FOR THOUGHT

The Main Ingredient

When faced with an overwhelming sense of stress, we have two
choices: we can either cling to the golden calf, or we can cling to our
Lord. If we make anything our god in this world, we are reshaping
our surroundings to be something it's not. There will never be anything that can heal, satisfy, or save like the Lord Jesus can.

A Slice of Advice

Dear Candace,

  *Do you have any recommendations that I can do spiritually wise,
in exercise, or nutritionally to reduce general anxiety? Whenever I get
anxious, my stomach gets upset.*

  Thanks and God bless,

—Liz

Dear Liz,

Absolutely! Obviously the first thing you can do is cut down on caffeine if you are drinking coffee or cola. Caffeine makes us all a bit edgy. Next up, you might be surprised to learn that carbohydrates can act as a tranquilizer to mellow you out. They increase the amount of serotonin in your brain, which is also something those suffering with depression are often lacking. Reach for complex carbohydrates that will last longer in your system such as fruit and whole-grain breads. Okay have a piece of dark chocolate too! Also consider taking a vitamin B supplement. B6 works to raise serotonin levels.

Don't let your blood sugar get too low. If you are hungry, you may get tense. If it's not time for dinner, a half ounce of juice can raise your blood sugar and keep you going until dinner.

Exercise relieves muscle tension so you feel more relaxed. Even if you only have time for some glute bridges, try to fit a workout in every day.

Some people are generally more prone to anxiety, and although we see it as something bad, it can be a very good thing. How we handle it is another. If you find that you're in a tough spot and you need to relax, lie down flat for a few minutes. Let the feeling of anxiety move through you, and thank God that He's made you this way. Allow yourself to feel what's going on in your body, knowing that God wired you this way for a purpose. Is your heart racing? Is your stomach growling? Let the feeling move through you freely. Don't try to fight it, just let it flow. It's God's work in progress healing your pain.

Start saying, "It is well with my soul." Just saying the words out loud sets your mind in a different direction.
—Candace

A Pinch of Practicality

Patience comes with patience. In other words, the more you exercise it, the more you obtain. We definitely weren't born patient;

in fact most of us came out kicking and screaming. But with guidance and—here's that word again—*patience* from our parents, we learned to wait, to tolerate, and to accept certain things—many things.

Mindfully tolerate the small things in life by biting your lip when need be, smiling under pressure, and forgiving others' imperfections. Try to exercise more of these moments throughout the day.

Place one hundred pennies in a cup on the counter. Each time you exercise patience throughout the day, move one penny from the full cup to the empty cup. The goal is to eventually move all of the pennies from one cup to the other. This exercise represents the giving of our self to others, as Christ has freely given to us.

Food for Thought

A recap of Scripture to meditate on:

- Do not be anxious about anything, but in everything, by prayer and petition, with thanksgiving, present your requests to God. And the peace of God, which transcends all understanding, will guard your hearts and your minds in Christ Jesus. (Phil. 4:6–7)
- What have you done to us by bringing us out of Egypt? Didn't we say to you in Egypt, "Leave us alone; let us serve the Egyptians"? It would have been better for us to serve the Egyptians than to die in the desert! (Exod. 14:11–12)
- Consider it pure joy, my brothers, whenever you face trials of many kinds, because you know that the testing of your faith develops perseverance. Perseverance must finish its work so that you may be mature and complete, not lacking anything. (James 1:2–4)

- These things happened to them as examples and were written down as warnings for us, on whom the fulfillment of the ages has come. So, if you think you are standing firm, be careful that you don't fall! No temptation has seized you except what is common to man. And God is faithful; he will not let you be tempted beyond what you can bear. But when you are tempted, he will also provide a way out so that you can stand up under it. (1 Cor. 10:11–13)

The Candy Dish

That which causes us trials shall yield us triumph: and that which make our hearts ache shall fill us with gladness. The only true happiness is to learn, to advance, and to improve: which could not happen unless we had comment with error, ignorance, and imperfection. We must pass through the darkness to reach the light. —Albert Pike

From My Stove to Yours

Fantastic Breakfast Oatmeal

Serves 2

INGREDIENTS

1 cup Old Fashioned Quaker Oats
1¾ cups of water
½ cup raisins
¼ canned pumpkin
2 tablespoons ground flaxseed
1 teaspoon cinnamon
¼ cup milk (optional)

DIRECTIONS

Combine water, raisins, and pumpkin and bring to a boil.

Stir oats into boiling mixture. Cook for 5 minutes over medium heat stirring occasionally.

Add flaxseed and cinnamon. Cover, remove from heat. Let stand until desired consistency. Spoon oatmeal into bowls.

Pour milk over oatmeal (optional).

SEVENTEEN

Is Meekness a Weakness?

Way back in the day, before diapers, bottles, and stretch marks, Val and I bought an adorable, yet mischievous, Valentine gift: Emma, a blonde Cocker Spaniel. We went to a breeder, hoping to adopt a pup, and that's where we first met her. There was something endearing about Emma; one look at her adoring hazel-colored eyes, long floppy ears, and playful disposition was enough for us to know she was ours.

We chose the name Emma because it had a romantic ring to it like Emily, but shortened, it rolled off the tongue. In fact, it was much easier to say, "Emma, get out of the garbage," or "Emma, get out of my purse" than it was to use all three syllables 162 times each day.

Emma could eat her way through a meat truck and still have a hankering for the gum in my purse. She loved her food and had no off button when she was full. We couldn't leave any leftovers on the table or she'd jump on the chair and devour everything. We couldn't place garbage anywhere near her, or she'd tip it over when we weren't looking and make her way through it. We couldn't hang candy canes on the Christmas tree unless we wanted to see the tree lying on its side the next day. She was definitely a food hound.

I remember one occasion when we had guests staying with us for a week. As per the norm, we briefed our guests on Emma, warning them not to leave one shred of food in their room. In addition to that, we instructed them to keep the door closed any time they were out, or Emma would make her way in.

"Are you sure you don't have food of any kind?" I asked. And they assured me they didn't.

Not realizing the potential that Emma had to sniff out and find food, our guests went out for the day, forgetting to close the bedroom door. They returned several hours later to find their suitcases open, clothing strewn around the room, makeup case unzipped, and an empty wrapper licked clean. That granola bar was never seen again.

I had to assure them that it wasn't our kids that got in there and ransacked their room. We had no doubt it was a little dog with a huge appetite and a lack of self-control.

We saw her do the same with purses. It wasn't uncommon for a friend to reach for her purse only to find the contents removed while Emma ran away with a piece of gum or a cough drop. She would open zippers, unsnap snaps, and unbuckle buckles to get her paws on a morsel of food.

Cocker spaniels are bred to hunt birds, and if they aren't exposed to the outlet for which they are born, they tend to be a little unbridled at times. I wasn't much of a bird hunter, nor had I planned to be, so Emma did her best to occupy herself with as much food as she could find. She could go from empty to way past full in sixty seconds flat. She got into garbage outside, she got into garbage inside, and she filled up on anything and everything she could find. She had the craziest appetite I've ever seen.

Each time she got caught, those remorseful eyes tried to convince me she would never do it again. But somehow I suspected she would.

Emma was fourteen years old last summer and by that age she was losing it. She was blind, deaf, and her quality of life was failing her, so with much sadness we decided to put her down.

Our little sweetheart was a curious, active dog with kitten-like paws and long floppy ears that reflected the free spirit she was. As much work as she was at times, I don't know if I'd have wanted her any other way.

In stark contrast to Emma was Sydney. She was a large breed dog with abundant strength. I got Sydney a short while before I moved out of my parents' house. She was my own dog and my responsibility. Our dad wasn't crazy about the idea of us getting a dog because he said that the responsibility of taking care of it would eventually fall on him. With all of us kids doing our own thing, he figured he'd be the one walking, feeding, and being the primary caretaker of the dog, and so we opted for reptiles instead. They weren't cuddly pets whatsoever, but they were easy to care for nonetheless.

Once I knew that I was getting my own house, my parents also agreed to let me get my own dog. I wanted a Rottweiler because of the security factor and also because I've always been drawn to that breed. Rottweilers are devoted, obedient, and eager to learn.

I went to a breeder to find her, and when the breeder saw how small I was, she was hesitant to sell me the male. That worked out best for me anyway because Sydney was my first choice. Unlike Emma (who came along later), Sydney was a calm and self-confident dog, who tested her surroundings before jumping in with four feet. Being a big dog, she preferred to live small, with a bark that was smaller than her bite. She was named after Laura Leighton's character, the fiery redhead on *Melrose Place*.

Her black and mahogany coat clothed a large muscular build—a ferocious appearance that was merely skin deep. People would often enter our property from the back to visit Mom's agency, but Sydney was gentle with everyone she met. We trained her to drop each time we said, "Bang!" Pointing my finger, she'd fall back with four paws in the air. It was a vulnerable position, especially for that type of dog. But Sydney was self-controlled and loyal at all times.

Once we moved out of Mom and Dad's place, Sydney's protective instincts gave me a sense of safety. Because of her exceptional strength, I was careful to bridle her energy with proper training and care. Alongside my efforts, I felt that Sydney put in great effort herself.

Sydney was with me when I moved out on my own, through my courtship with Val, and through the birth of all three of our children. Her protective instincts made her a great family pet alongside Emma.

There were times when we were living in Montreal, Canada, when Val was playing hockey with the Canadiens that I had to board her back in California at my parents' house. Val was on the road a lot, and if I was busy, she would stay there for months at a time. California was always her home away from home. And as much as my dad tried to avoid it, the responsibility of taking care of a dog eventually did fall back on him. But my parents loved Sydney and could hardly resist such a well-trained companion, who really wasn't much work.

She was gentle with our children and protective when she needed to be. With Val traveling, the kids and I were often alone. We appreciated having a large protective dog in the house. She was better security than any alarm system could offer.

I'd often say, "If anyone wants to break in my house, they have to deal with my dogs."

Sydney could sit, roll, and lie down on command. And she would twist and perk up her triangular ears when we asked, "Who's there?" She was good on a leash. Meanwhile Emma would walk alongside her distracted by the scent of anything that even slightly smelled edible.

She was a remarkable companion who shared a good part of our lives. Unfortunately she was only ten when she got cancer and soon after died in surgery.

When I think of Sydney and Emma, I see the contrast in their personalities, and I discover the benefit that meekness can add to one's character. I've found a deeper understanding of meekness and how to apply it to my life. Suddenly its purpose is clear.

Is meekness a weakness? Often we equate the word *meekness* with words like:

- Weak
- Timid
- Nervous
- Shy
- Frail
- Feeble
- Hesitant

Yet when we look closer at the word *meek*, we find strength under control.

The Greek word is *praeiv*, translated in *Strong's Concordance* (#4239) as: "mildness of disposition, gentleness of spirit, meekness." True synonyms for the word *meek* include:

- Humble
- Submissive

- Gentle
- Obedient
- Subservient
- Modest
- Mild

So the idea is that a meek person is someone who is gentle, tolerant, patient, long-suffering, and someone who is submissive to God.

> *Blessed are the meek, for they shall inherit the earth.*
> *(Matt. 5:5)*

Contrary to the way the world would see it, meekness does not equate weakness. In fact, it's the exact opposite. Meekness is being strong yet controlled.

When studying the Word, I found that the Greeks often equated meekness with the taming of an animal, such as a horse that was broken in as opposed to one that is wild. This reminded me so much of Sydney. With incredible body strength, she was capable of doing severe damage, and yet she was the meekest animal I have ever met. We knew she was meek each time she rolled over on her back and played dead. It was one of the most submissive actions an animal of her breed could display.

By the time Sydney was a few years old, she was trained to respond well on a leash. While we took her for walks alongside Emma, she quietly kept pace. Emma on the other hand wanted the world to know she was there. She liked to be heard and be seen. When approached by other dogs, Sydney remained calm. Knowing she could take most dogs out with one gulp, she chose not to strike back. Instead of retaliating, she remained under control, following the lead of her master.

I look to Jesus whose life was a reflection of His desire to follow the Master. He always put the Father's will over His. When He was tempted in the desert, He stayed calm and continued His work. When He was driven out of town by an angry mob who threatened to throw Him off a cliff, He chose to leave calmly. He could have called a multitude of angels to His rescue, He could have let emotion overshadow the plan, but He didn't. He remained controlled under pressure—the essence of meekness.

> *He was oppressed and afflicted,*
> *yet he did not open his mouth;*
> *he was led like a lamb to the slaughter,*
> *and as a sheep before her shearers is silent,*
> *so he did not open his mouth. (Isa. 53:7)*

And the same meek and gentle Jesus Christ:

> *Entered the temple area and drove out all who were buying and selling there. He overturned the tables of the money changers and the benches of those selling doves. (Matt. 21:12)*

How is that meek?

Always ready to defend His faith yet never defending Himself. Therein lays the strength of the meek: in the ability to control one's passions and desires. There is a time when defense is in order, and in the case of the money changers, Jesus was illustrating that lesson. He never defended himself, but He was always ready to defend the Father.

Sydney and Emma depicted both meekness and weakness. One was led by unbridled passion while the other was strength under control.

If we learn to control our passions in the small things of life, we equip ourselves to be further controlled in the larger issues.

On the other hand, if we let our emotions rule us, we become a slave to them.

We know it's not good to eat too much food or to indulge in junk just because our body craves the sugar and salt. Each time we do, we exercise that same uncontrolled passion that Emma displayed. If we don't rule our passions, we leave ourselves open and vulnerable to attack.

Jesus equipped Himself for ministry by fasting in the wilderness for forty days and forty nights, bringing His body under subjection to the Spirit. Can you say no to an extra brownie or two? Can you say no to a soda pop and grab water instead? Each time you let your passions rule your choice, you are letting them rule over you. Isn't that a discouraging thought?

Can you imagine how great a force we could be if we could live a life of meekness in the same manner as Jesus? If we could bridle our passion to where the Spirit is taking the lead, we could become a conquering force able not only to reject the next binge but to stand up for our faith when the going gets tough.

If controlling our appetite weren't of great importance, why would fasting be of any use? It's a form of self-denial, and any healthy denial of self teaches our flesh that God's Spirit is in control.

Losing weight is great, but the truth is that our pant size isn't what bugs us the most, is it? It's our failure to control our appetite time and time again. It's the overwhelming feeling that we're in bondage to food. It's the feeling that we're trapped in a body that has control over us. That's why we want change. That's why we need change!

When we're self-controlled, we eat until we are satisfied. We exercise because we know it's a good thing to do. And we make healthy choices because we are following a plan instead of a whim.

Is meekness a weakness? Not a chance. It's bridled passion under control.

The Pantry

CHOCKED-FULL OF FOOD FOR THOUGHT

The Main Ingredient

One of the greatest characteristics anyone could possess is the ability to control their passion. Following a plan instead of yielding to impulse keeps us on a sure and steady path to freedom.

A Slice of Advice

Candace,

I know that you love Pilates and that they've been great in keeping your stomach flat. I saw you on VH1's celebrity slim-downs, and you looked fantastic. I couldn't believe you have three kids and still look like you're twenty!

I'd love to try Pilates, but I don't even know what it's all about. Do you know of any online resources that have good Pilates videos, or of any DVDs I can pick up to do Pilates at home? Also, is this something that I actually can do at home, or would I need special equipment the gym would provide?

I'd love to give this a shot.

—Merrilee

Hi Merrilee,

I was introduced to Pilates by my neighbor who lost her last twenty pounds and kept bugging me to go with her. She told me how much I'd love it and wouldn't want to do anything else. She was right! I go to a *studio where they have Pilates equipment, which includes a reformer, a chair, and the tower.*

I've found that in doing Pilates over the years, I find the results to be much better in a studio with an instructor than on a DVD with just a mat on the floor. I'm sure if a studio isn't convenient for you, DVDs would be a good option. The equipment itself is pricey, and unless you're totally dedicated to it, I can't imagine anyone purchasing it as a beginner, although I know there are some alternative products for in-home use.

One thing I'd like to add is that if you find a studio, make sure the instructor is teaching you proper technique, aligning and adjusting your body so you can feel your muscles working, and instructing so you're sweating through the session. Many Pilates teachers can instruct in a slow, stretching type of technique, and as a woman who wants a good workout, this style isn't for me. I need to be pushed and move at a faster, harder rate.

Hope that helps!
—Candace

A Pinch of Practicality

If treats or bonus points are a part of your healthy plan, try to save them for the end of the day when possible. It's always nice to have something to look forward to. However, if we consume our rewards too early in the day, we might give in to a feeling of deprivation. It's always nice to feel that balance when we have had a good day and can rest assured that enjoying a treat is a guilt-free snack.

Be cautious that you don't overindulge. Choose your portion beforehand and stick to your rule. Enjoy every bite, and remember that it's still going to be there tomorrow.

Food for Thought

A recap of Scripture to meditate on:

- Blessed are the meek, for they shall inherit the earth. (Matt. 5:5)
- He was oppressed and afflicted,
  yet he did not open his mouth;
  he was led like a lamb to the slaughter,
  and as a sheep before her shearers is silent,
  so he did not open his mouth. (Isa. 53:7)
- Jesus entered the temple area and drove out all who were buying and selling there. He overturned the tables of the money changers and the benches of those selling doves. (Matt. 21:12)

The Candy Dish

The meek man is not a human mouse afflicted with a sense of his own inferiority. Rather he may be in his moral life as bold as a lion and as strong as Samson; but he has stopped being fooled about himself. He has accepted God's estimate of his own life. —A. W. Tozer

Oven Roasted Broccoli

Serves 4

INGREDIENTS

   1 pound broccoli, rinsed and trimmed

   2 tablespoons olive oil

   2 cloves garlic, minced

   ½ teaspoon kosher salt

   ¼ teaspoon freshly ground black pepper

   ⅓ cup Panko bread crumbs

   ¼ cup finely grated Parmesan or sharp Cheddar

DIRECTIONS

Combine, oil, garlic, kosher salt, and pepper. Cut the broccoli into bite-sized pieces and coat with the oil mixture.

   Spread the Panko bread crumbs into a 13 x 9-inch cake pan, and toast it in the oven for about two minutes. Remove from the oven and add the bread crumbs to the broccoli mixture, coating the broccoli well. Place the coated broccoli in the cake pan and roast at 425 degrees until tender (about 8 to 10 minutes).

   Remove from the oven, toss with cheese, and serve. You'll love it!

EIGHTEEN

Leaving a Legacy

If you are married with children, or hope to be in the future, this chapter's for you. It's my goal to encourage parents to leave a legacy for their children that includes more than our worldly possessions. In addition to the morals and faith we instill, we can train them to understand and care for their bodies.

When I think about that, I'm reminded of the characters on *Make It or Break It*. The extensive preparation they go through for each routine is necessary to prevent them from stumbling, or worse—breaking their neck. It involves strength training, concentration and balance—three things we all need to learn.

Summer, my character on the show, is a Christian, but I still have to remind some fans that she's not me. There are certainly things about her that are similar to me and the way I live out my faith, while some things are not. We have the same hair, the same eyes, and the same smile, but our characters aren't alike. It's a difficult separation for some viewers, and a job I try to monitor and discern wisely.

In the same manner I have to discern wisely when it comes to our children and the television programming they watch. I know that many of you were looking forward to another *Full House*, but haven't found it there. Frankly, I'd love it if this was a show that every member of my family could sit down and watch, but *Make It or Break It* is a "teen" drama with a rating of +14.

When we started taping the show it was exciting for my kids to see their mom back on TV. They got to come to the set with me to see how things were unfolding back stage. Natasha got to meet all my co-stars, while Maks and Lev peered through the lens of a real television camera and helped the director yell "action." They got to see where Mom gets that glowing skin that only a talented director of photography and great make-up artist can give, and they tiptoed on balance beams in between takes.

I do allow Natasha to watch the show since it's right up her ally as a budding teen. But as a concerned and involved parent, we watch together, remote in my hand so I can fast forward through any parts I feel are a bit too mature for her to see. And as for the boys, well, they're perfectly happy watching Monday night football instead!

My job as a mom is to nurture and train each little spirit, body, and soul till they're grown, protecting what their eyes see, what their ears hear, and what food they're stuffing into their mouth. My job as their coach is to provide strength training, concentration, and balance until their ready to step out on their own. So when Val and I realized that the schools weren't offering the most nutritious meals to our kids, we made a conscious effort to start packing lunches that would.

Roast beef, ham, or turkey sandwiches on whole wheat are always a good option, and, yeah, I'm also a peanut butter and jelly mom too! The juice box is something I loved as a kid, and it's still something I like today, so I'll rotate juice, water and milk, switching it up so they don't drink sugar every day.

Any mom with boys knows how much they love to wrestle and roll, so fruit doesn't always wear well when Maks and Lev are carrying it around. By lunch time the bananas look like they confronted Mike Tyson and the pears, Muhammad Ali. So I got creative and found some alternatives. The supermarket sells sliced and prepackaged fruit, and the apples don't turn brown. These are a hit—not a "right hook," but a big hit nonetheless! I might also peel oranges, breaking them apart and grapes are always a good option too.

It's hard for some families to get past the habits they've had, but with a little concentration, you can find a lot of snacks that are fun and much healthier than potato chips. Snacks like a hundred calorie cookies, air-popped popcorn, organic Oreos, Goldfish crackers, and string cheese are just a few of the other ideas I've had. They also love celery with fresh-ground almond butter or baby carrots with a side of ranch dressing. And once in a while, I'll stop at Subway and get them a sandwich and chocolate milk, but that's usually if I didn't have time to go to the grocery store and get my shopping done.

If we are training our bodies, it's so important that we train our kids as well. Not that we're putting them on a diet but that they're learning what types of food are good for them. What are carbohydrates? What are proteins? What are sugars, and what types are good for you? What types of fats are good, and how much should you eat? These are the questions we should be providing the answers to. It's good for us to know, but it's equally important that we teach our children.

If we simply deny them, it won't go far without the knowledge as to *why*. Teach them why they should have a balanced meal with protein, carbs, vegetables, grains, and fats. Help them understand if they are going to play sports then they should learn that carbohydrates and a little protein help us fuel up for rigorous exercise.[2]

Again, it's not about denying our kids ice cream or cake but rather training them to eat these foods in moderation. Portion size must be learned. Are they going for seconds or thirds because it tastes great, or do they really require more food?

Here's the difference. Although I did have some good instruction, I didn't know how to eat properly growing up. It was one extreme or another for us. Remember how I said Dad was into cardboard-tasting yet healthy food while Mom was sneaking doughnuts and ice cream our way? I believe that's why I struggled with weight. I wasn't trained to understand the importance of balance, nor was I strong enough to make healthy choices.

I want to pass a legacy down to my children that equips them to excel, but I know that in order to do this I have to live a compelling life that draws my children to live the same way. I look to the Bible for example where I see a young widow named Ruth, who is so drawn to the life of her mother-in-law, Naomi. One can only wonder what powerful effect Naomi had on Ruth that made her so willing to leave her own people and faith to follow her.

> But Ruth replied, "Don't urge me to leave you or to turn back from you. Where you go I will go, and where you stay I will stay. Your people will be my people and your God my God. Where you die I will die, and there I will be buried. May the LORD deal with me, be it ever so severely, if anything but death separates you and me." (Ruth 1:16–17)

Naomi must have been a woman of virtue and strength to have made such an impact on Ruth's life that she was willing to desert her own people to follow her. I strive to be that compelling force in my family so that I can offer the best life possible for them. That must include the way I eat and the way I exercise. I don't want to see my kids struggling with yoyo diets as I did. I'm not saying they won't, but at least I'm giving them a good start by offering an example as well as implementing it into their lives.

Teach them along the way, both at home and when dining out. If they go to a restaurant, what are some good choices and what portion size should they eat? Get involved by discussing the menu with them instead of leaving it to their choice. Maybe you could offer them three healthy choices instead of sending them straight to the kids menu for chicken fingers and fries.

We are a guiding light to our families, so if we're keeping our healthy eating plan under wraps, it's kind of like hiding the light that could otherwise have a huge impact on their lives.

> You are the light of the world. A city on a hill cannot be hidden. Neither do people light a lamp and put it under a bowl. Instead they put it on its stand, and it gives light to everyone in the house. In the same way, let your light shine before men, that they may see your good deeds and praise your Father in heaven. (Matt. 5:14–16)

Food shouldn't be viewed as an enemy or as a temptation they can't have. We can eat all things; we just need to learn when and how much. Food is fuel for the body and can be enjoyed, but it shouldn't become a stronghold in their lives or mine.

Practically speaking to all you moms making dinner on a diet: get it out of your brain that your kids should be eating macaroni and cheese while you have grilled salmon and broccoli. Face the fact that you're in this together. There are so many wonderful foods to share with them regardless of whether they like it from the start or not.

Lev doesn't like tomatoes and onions, so if I make something for dinner, I'll reserve a little that doesn't have those ingredients, but I won't make him an entirely different dinner. I introduce new foods to them often to expand their palette.

Check out the recipes I've included in "The Pantry." Maybe you don't typically eat eggplant or Brussels sprouts, and if not maybe it's time for a change.

Try a new recipe, and let your kids try it too. The rule of thumb in my family is to at least try it. If you don't like it, you don't have to eat the whole thing, but you do have to try one bite. And you know what? More times than not, they think it will be gross, but they like it! Sometimes they don't and that's fine too. But at some point I will ask them to try it again. Their palette will grow over time if you continue to introduce new foods to them. You will be surprised at the things they will like, especially when they see Mom and Dad enjoying them too. My kids love roasted asparagus, and they love the cauliflower with anchovies recipe that I've included in this chapter. We have introduced such a variety of foods to our children over the years, developing their palette, it's no wonder people ask me how I get my children to eat the things they do and enjoy them.

Listen up, you picky eaters! Don't pass your limited palette down to your children. It's another way of setting them up for failure with food. I want to encourage Moms and Dads to step out of your comfort zone, even if you don't normally like something, and try making it for yourselves and the kids. Then try it again next month, and be consistent about it because taste buds change over time.

Val is the chef in our family who can cook a beautifully fantastic meal, but as a busy working mom who doesn't share a passion for the kitchen, I need to make simple things with few ingredients. I've included our family favorites—things we consistently make and eat. Don't gag just yet, but the cauliflower recipe is my all-time favorite! Most people find cauliflower bland because we only know it raw alongside ranch dressing on a veggie tray, but there are so many other ways to prepare it! Cauliflower soup, cauliflower mash, cauliflower gratin. . . . Can't you just hear my excitement?! The cauliflower anchovy recipe at the end of this chapter sounds disgusting, I know, but there's no fishy taste, I promise. It's a wonderful salty, roasted flavor that you'll be wanting more of, and you can indulge because it's so good for you! Try it.

I've also included pork chops and turkey meatloaf—two others that are tasty and simple to make that your whole family will love. Veggies get so little attention, so I have included a few ideas to make as a side dish or to have as your main meal.

You'll also sense a little bit of a Mexican theme with some of these recipes. I've included enchiladas, fajitas, and turkey tacos. Being raised in LA, there is a big Mexican influence, which we happily encourage when it comes to food. Huevos rancheros anyone? But I'm sure by now you've noticed that we love all kinds of food.

Good health is a lifestyle choice our whole family has made. The good choices that Val and I make are the same options we offer our children when it comes to their health. Our diet is no different from theirs.

I encourage you to eat wholesome food. If it's something you eat in moderation, they should too. If you cut out fast food, it's not wise to make trips there just for the kids. It should be reserved for a treat or a special time. So while you are training your kids to make the smart decision on their own, you're also teaching them self-control.

Another thing we need to share with our family is fitness. Heart health is vital, which is why my kids are active in sports. Exercise is incredibly important and an essential part of life. This is something Val's family passed down to him, and we are now passing down to our children.

During the school year our kids play sports. Lev and Maks are currently playing hockey, Natasha joined the track and field team at school, and all three kids play tennis. Hockey is not something I'm on the ice doing with them, but tennis and running are activities I can play or do alongside them. They get excited when I race down the street or play a game of tennis, especially since they have gotten so good and can beat me.

During the summer we play sports together a whole lot more. I get a break from work, and they are out of school. Since we're only three blocks from the beach, all five of us will go there for a run. About four times a week, we run thirty to forty-five minutes together. I love the smiles from people as they pass-by team Bure!

We also do our beach exercises in the sand. Maks loves to throw the frisbee, Lev likes to play football, and we all enjoy boogie and skim boarding together. It keeps us active while we're having a blast! Maybe you don't live near the beach, but if you live near a park, you can always go there to play football or soccer. Use trees or shoes as goalposts. There are so many fun, creative ways to enjoy your children and exercise with them.

We bike ride too. In Florida we'd take a great route near our house that went through an enormous park, but now that we're back in LA, the beach path it is. The path goes from our house through Santa Monica and Pacific Palisades. Not only are we teaching our kids good exercise habits, but it's working for us too.

You don't have to be sweating it out at the gym alone. Life is about living. A mom can be overwhelmed thinking about how to find time to work, exercise, run errands, prepare dinner, do the laundry, and spend quality time with the kids after school while they do homework. But if you think about it, you can spend time with kids outside getting fresh air and exercising together while dinner's cooking in the oven. How's that for multitasking? If you are a list person like me, you can check off a few things at once:

❑ Dinner
❑ Exercise
❑ Spending time with the children
❑ Teaching good habits.

It's done, all in one shot! It should feel less overwhelming when there is a practical way to exercise with the family. This kind of behavior draws our children's attention and peaks their interest in us. Once we have their attention, we can instill the value of health that they can carry for years. All it takes is a little strength training, concentration, and balance—three things we all need to learn. Exercise will encourage activity and an interest in sports, which leads to good health. Be that compelling person your family needs you to be, and start letting that little light shine!

The Pantry
CHOCKED-FULL OF FOOD FOR THOUGHT

The Main Ingredient

Healthy food shouldn't be reserved for moms and dads on a diet. If you are making better choices for your life, you should be making them for your child as well. Good health should be a family affair, a legacy we pass down to our kids.

Slice of Advice

Dear Candace

Candace, I want to ask if you have any thoughts about how to teach our little ones about Christ? I have two boys: ages two and five. I try to teach them about God; we read Bible stories at bedtime, and we pray and talk about God here and there. Maybe it's just a developmental thing, but my five-year-old seems so aloof. When he prays, he's just repeating the words he's heard me pray; it doesn't come from within himself. And when I try to teach him about God, he's looking off into space or trying to play with something. It is so frustrating to me because more than anything I want them to know and love the Lord.

I'm not sure if God is just still an abstract idea to him or if he just doesn't have a reverence for God yet. Would love to know your thoughts! Thanks so much!

—Delanie

Dear Delanie,

You sound like you are doing a wonderful job with your children teaching them about Christ. Don't be discouraged if your five-year-old doesn't "get" Him yet—he's five! Yes, I know some children who have professed their love for the Lord at the same age, but everyone develops differently. The most important thing you can continue to do is to love your children and teach them about God. Continue to read with them, play with them, and nurture them. Don't think that reading those Bible stories is all for nothing. You'll be surprised one day when your son is asked about something and he'll recall a Bible story mommy read. Kids are like sponges. They soak it ALL in. Some kids just don't squeeze it out till later.

I love The Way of the Master book for kids. It's a really fun way to learn the Ten Commandments and the story of creation. Remember that the best way to teach your kids at a young age about God, is to reflect within yourself the things you're trying to teach. In other words, live out your life for Christ. Your actions will speak loud and clear.

Keep up the good work and put your worry to rest. God loves your boys more than you do! Can you imagine that?!

—Candace

A Pinch of Practicality

When you take your kids out for ice cream or a doughnut, walk there with them. The first time our friends took their kids, Blake and Chloe, out for a doughnut, it took them a good twenty-five minutes to get there. They grumbled a bit. But they enjoyed the doughnut enough that they wanted to go again the next week.

The treat is worth the effort. Get them to ride their bikes or a scooter if it's a little farther for them. Or get the whole family to grocery shop together and each carry a bag home. That will also teach some good manners.

Another practical tip I can offer is that I purposely hand my boys the groceries every time I check out of the store, or I'll stop in front of the doors to wait for them to open it, so they'll learn how to treat a lady well.

Food for Thought

A recap of Scripture to meditate on:

- But Ruth replied, "Don't urge me to leave you or to turn back from you. Where you go I will go, and where you stay I will stay. Your people will be my people and your God my God. Where you die I will die, and there I will be buried. May the LORD deal with me, be it ever so severely, if anything but death separates you and me." (Ruth 1:16–17)
- You are the light of the world. A city on a hill cannot be hidden. Neither do people light a lamp and put it under a bowl. Instead they put it on its stand, and it gives light to everyone in the house. In the same way, let your light shine before men, that they may see your good deeds and praise your Father in heaven. (Matt. 5:14–16)

The Candy Dish

"*Children are the seeds our days plant.*" —*Anne Voskamp*

From My Stove to Yours

Cauliflower Sauteed with Anchovies

Not a big fan of cauliflower or anchovies? Just trust me on this one and try it at least once. There is no fishy taste, but it's salty and fantastic!

It's my all-time FAVORITE!

Serves 4 as a side, or I eat the whole thing for dinner.

INGREDIENTS

1 medium head cauliflower
3 tablespoons olive oil
4 to 6 anchovy fillets, drained
Pepper to taste
Water, if needed

DIRECTIONS

Wash the cauliflower and break it into small florets; also chop the stems. Heat a large skillet over medium high. Sauté the oil and anchovies in a skillet—just until you see the anchovies have broken down. Add the cauliflower. Season with pepper and stir to coat.

Cook on high heat for about 20 minutes (adding a little water if you need to so it doesn't brown too fast). Turn the heat down to low and cover for about 5 minutes or until cauliflower is tender.

NINETEEN

Being Good Isn't Good Enough

Do you trust God enough to enter His rest?

Take a look at this verse, and let it soak in for a minute:

I gave up all that inferior stuff so I could know Christ person-ally, experience his resurrection power, be a partner in his suffering, and go all the way with him to death itself. If there was any way to get in on the resurrection from the dead, I wanted to do it. I'm not saying that I have this all together, that I have it made. But I am well on my way, reaching out for Christ, who has so wondrously reached out for me. (Phil. 3:10–12 The Message)

Paul wasn't merely hoping to experience the resurrection of Jesus Christ; he was also willing to be a partner in the sufferings of Christ. When we look at the trials Jesus faced throughout His life, and even more so on the day of His crucifixion, we see: grief, fear, shame, regret, hunger, thirst, wrath, terror, judgment, and death.

Christ's vigorous journey to the cross and His obedience to the Father remind me to "let go and let God." The Bible refers to this letting go as entering into His rest, "Let us, therefore, make every effort to enter that rest, so that no one will fall by following their example of disobedience" (Heb. 4:11).

Rest and the cross—can the two be compared? Absolutely—let me explain why. When we enter His rest, we give up our fight. His hand takes over and begins to animate our lives like the shell of a puppet. It's not easy to put down our will so that His can be done. It's not easy to face shame for His sake or judgment or terror, but we might when we choose God's will over ours for our lives.

What about hunger and thirst? Do you know that hunger is a running theme throughout the Scriptures? God fed the Israelites on manna for forty years to teach them that He alone sustains life. Complete dependency on Him is the eternal lesson we all must learn. Dependency = rest. Again we see this complete dependency from Jesus Himself in John 19:

> Later, knowing that all was now completed, and so that the Scripture would be fulfilled, Jesus said, "I am thirsty." A jar of wine vinegar was there, so they soaked a sponge in it, put the sponge on a stalk of the hyssop plant, and lifted it to Jesus' lips. When he had received the drink, Jesus said, "It is finished." With that, he bowed his head and gave up his spirit. (vv. 28–30)

When I look at lessons like that, my diet—my struggle to eat well and move more, to stop when I'm full—pales in comparison. It's just one thing of many that I had to hand over to God in my life.

Let me paint a scenario. You've eaten a good dinner, stopped when you were satisfied, and feel pretty good about the choices you've made. Thirty minutes later the TV goes on, and the family starts rummaging through the kitchen for a television snack. Suddenly you get the munchies. Your brain starts off slow and then goes into a wild frenzy of arguments giving you every reason you deserve to eat more than you should. Telling you that you can break the rules "just this once" even though you know that last night, and the night before that and the night before that, were the "just once" days too.

Say "no."

What's the worst that can happen? You suffer a little internal sting while others around you indulge. As Paul said, make every effort to enter into His rest, which includes the resolution that God and only God can sustain us.

Making it through the little lessons helps to strengthen us for the tougher ones: grief, fear, shame, regret, wrath, terror, judgment, and death. It's not easy to put down our will so that His can be done, but I promise you this: it will bring peace to your life.

In all areas of my life I continue to put down my will for His. That includes health, family, friends, and work. Working in television and movies today can be difficult for a Christian, and at times it's difficult to know where to draw the line and when it's okay to say yes. That's when I use conscience and prayer to decide.

I've worked on a few things that I have regretted since becoming a Christian. There's no turning back. However, now that I have a biblical worldview, my decisions are different, and my options are fewer. Some agents will tell new actors that they can't be picky about what they work on if they intend to establish themselves. In fact, many of them will push actors to audition for everything and will encourage them to take whatever is available. There's no doubt that acting jobs aren't increasing with the takeover of reality television. They'll tell you not to worry about compromising on the small stuff now because if you start working regularly and develop a name for yourself, you will have more opportunity to pick and choose then.

Entering into His rest means that I MUST pick and choose. I don't want to compromise my moral standards for some time in front of the camera. And I certainly won't work on something that could lead any searching soul astray, or as Paul says, fall by my example of disobedience. This has made it difficult to be a Christian in the entertainment business at times.

Many TV shows and movies today don't uphold the standards I value as a Christian and as a mom. I am blessed to work with managers and an agency that are fully aware of where I stand morally, who know that I won't go on auditions if they compromise my faith in any way. Honestly, it's not easy to find those people who are willing to work like this when there are so many other talented actors who are willing to take any and all roles.

If an audition comes along and there isn't much information on it, I get the sides in advance so I can decide either to take it or pass, just as I do with Natasha.

I hope I can be like the apostle Paul one day who WANTS to partake in the sufferings of Christ. I want to live in obedience, but there's always a part of me that hopes that obedience will turn in my favor. Being putty in His hands, resting in His plans, and laying my burden at His feet means that I'll be a different wife, mom, daughter, friend, and actor than the world would expect. It means that I'll be animated by the hand of my Lord, ready to do His will when He speaks. I can't be salt and light if I become like everyone else.

God has placed me in a position that's wonderful most days, but at other times it's a sobering place to be. I realize that being in front of the camera on national television, standing on stage in front of an audience of ten thousand people, and being a mom to my three little kids are all tasks that come with enormous responsibility. I don't take any of them lightly. As a Christian I know that the day will come when I stand in front of my Lord and give account for every word that was spoken. I pray His response will be "Well done, my good and faithful Candace."

> But I tell you that men will have to give account on the day of judgment for every careless word they have spoken. For by your words you will be acquitted, and by your words you will be condemned. (Matt. 12:36–37)

The idea of entering His rest is confusing at times. On one hand we're instructed to cease from our labor, and then James 2:20 tells us, "You foolish man, do you want evidence that faith without deeds is useless?" So what gives? Do we work, or do we rest?

I have a line of T-shirts, and one of the best sellers reads, "Being Good Isn't Good Enough." It makes people look when they see it because it would seem that I'm expecting perfection, when in fact that's not what it's saying at all. It's a great conversation piece to get chatting about the Lord.

If you think you're a good person, you should ask yourself, "Am I good enough to go to heaven?" The answer to that is found when we measure ourselves against the principles of the Ten Commandments found in Exodus 20:

1. You shall have no other gods before Me.
2. You shall not make for yourself an idol in the form of anything.
3. You shall not misuse the name of the LORD your God.
4. Remember the Sabbath day, to keep it holy.
5. Honor your father and your mother.
6. You shall not murder.
7. You shall not commit adultery.
8. You shall not steal.

9. You shall not give false testimony about your neighbor.

10. You shall not covet.

I've broken all of those Ten Commandments. And if I'm certain of one thing, it's that you've broken them too. "But Candace," you're saying, "I haven't murdered anyone." And unless you're sitting on death row right now reading this book, I get your point. But Jesus explained that if you as much as hate your brother, you are guilty of murder because God sees the thoughts and intents of our heart. By that standard I know I'm a sinner, and it sends me to the One who paid my fine for the moral law I have violated so many times. As I kneel at the foot of the blood-stained cross, I know that I'm saved by grace and grace alone. My salvation has nothing to do with my goodness because in the light of that holy law, I don't have any. My freedom is paid for by the blood of Jesus Christ. I could never be "good enough" to enter heaven on my merit alone, but because I lean on Jesus as the author of my faith, I am animated by His will.

When I think of entering into His rest, I imagine myself lifeless waiting for the hand of God to bring me to life. I think of myself an empty shell ready to be moved by His will when it is no longer me who's living but God who is living through me. When God lives through us, "it is God who works in you to will and to act according to his good purpose" (Phil. 2:13). That is where works by faith come in.

Even Jesus Himself gave up His will in Matthew 26:39, "Going a little farther, he fell with his face to the ground and prayed, 'My Father, if it is possible, may this cup be taken from me. Yet not as I will, but as you will.'" In fact, the entire life of Christ was to do the will of the Father.

Another T-shirt I have in my collection is "Growing in God." If you see my Web site, you'll notice that "Growing in God" is a running theme in my life. Millions of people watched me grow up in front of their eyes on television, and now I'd like you to watch me continue growing in faith.

Some Christians in Hollywood don't share their faith. Others, like my brother Kirk and me, want nothing more than to let our faith shine. We've taken a public stand. Not only because Jesus tells us to, but because our hearts have been convicted of our sin and the urgency to warn others. There are no second chances. "It is appointed for men to die once, but after this the judgment" (Heb. 9:27 NKJV).

Jesus said in Matthew 28:18–20: "All authority in heaven and on earth has been given to me. Therefore go and make disciples of all nations, baptizing them in the name of the Father and of the Son and of the Holy Spirit, and teaching them to obey everything I have commanded you. And surely I am with you always, to the very end of the age."

To illustrate this point, I'd like you to imagine that you are a scientist and you have discovered the cure for cancer. Millions of people in the world are dying of cancer, so what do you do? Simple. You give people the cure you discovered so they also can live. See, this cure shows the urgency in the need for the cure.

It's the same thing with sharing the gospel; people are dying every day without knowing the Lord. These people will spend eternity separated from God in hell. But we as Christians have the "cure." We know who can save these people from hell, and that cure is Jesus. We need to point people to Jesus so they can live too.

I have so many great fans who have supported me over the years, through my days on *Full House*, and now as they watch me play Summer on *Make It or Break It*! Many have witnessed a change in me and have heard me freely talk about my faith. Sometimes the reaction is good, and sometimes it isn't so pleasant. People are going to expect me to be the same person I've always been, but when the Lord saved me and I became a new creation in Christ, I started growing in God.

It isn't always easy to stand strong in my faith, especially when I know that many in the media are waiting for me to slip up, for me to give reason for ridicule. But nevertheless, I do it because it's God's will for my life. Because I live an integrated Christian life, my walk with Him penetrates all aspects of my life. That includes my family, finances, work, relationships, my thoughts . . . everything. God wants all of me, including the Candace I am at work, not just the Candace that goes to church on Sundays or tells Bible stories in the privacy of her home. No matter how long I've been a Christian, I continue to pray that the Lord will rule in every area of my life.

God has changed me in ways words can't describe. He has transformed the way I think and live my life. Things that were once important to me are no longer vital. I can't help but share the good news with everyone! I know nothing is more important, and I know that without Christ the eternal consequences are devastating. I urge you to surrender your whole life to Jesus, turn from your sin, and trust in Him with all your heart. Pick up a Bible, and start reading it now. Let me leave you with this:

> *"And the times of this ignorance God winked at: but now commands all men every where to repent: because he has appointed a day, in the which he will judge the world in righteousness by that man whom he has ordained."* (Acts 17:30–31)

Let's close this book in prayer together . . .

Dear Lord,

Thank You for teaching me the divine lessons of self-discipline. I pray that as I practice each lesson, I'll cherish its worth in place of my goal. Help me find the strength to live a self-disciplined life at all times. Help me discern where I need to change and to exercise my will when the going gets tough. Thank you for the struggles I face and the fruit that each triumph brings into my life.

Give me strength when I'm teaching my body to yield and Your divine Spirit when I need wisdom to lead. Give me examples of people to follow so that I too can learn. Show me ways I should change and give me the insight to do it.

Help me make life-changing choices that not only grow me as a person but also impact the world that I affect every day. Help me to obey Your Word, as my heart guides my head.

Teach me contentment in all that I do, so that I can say with all certainty, "It is well with my soul."

Amen.

The Pantry
CHOCKED-FULL OF FOOD FOR THOUGHT

The Main Ingredient

Walking in faith isn't always the easiest path, especially when the world holds so much distraction for us. But if we want to live a victorious life that is free from the pull of the world, we need to include God in all that we do. God doesn't call us to be "good." He calls us to repentance through His Son Jesus Christ. And through that repentance we desire to serve.

Hi Candace,

When it comes to sharing my faith, sometimes I prefer just to act as an example, or "love on people," because I have trouble putting God's love into words. How do you share your faith without appearing condescending, judgmental, or preachy?

—Jenna

Dear Jenna,

Great question! It can be so hard and intimidating to share our faith with others. I'm not nearly as bold as I'd like to be at times and imagine that I've missed many opportunities. I always try to act out my faith by example and to be loving in all my actions. That simply is the fruit that's given to us by the Holy Spirit when we've received Christ.

But the Bible tells us to go into the world and make disciples. This isn't just something for evangelists to do or for us to do if we feel called to share the gospel. Mark 16:15–16 says "[Jesus] said to them, 'Go into all the world and preach the good news to all creation. Whoever believes and is baptized will be saved, but whoever does not believe will be condemned.'"

This is an urgent message for all believers. That last sentence is the reason we MUST share our faith. I highly recommend: One Thing You Can't Do In Heaven *by Mark Cahill. This book will equip you with ideas for starting conversations, examples of witnessing situations, and answers to common questions.*

Don't be intimidated to start a conversation because you think you won't know all the answers. Chances are, you won't. But you can always say, "I don't know. But I'd love to find out the answer to that and get back to you." And DO!

Sharing your faith with someone doesn't need to turn judgmental or preachy. In love, you can develop some methods to start up a dialogue *by simply asking questions to get others thinking. Just remember, it's all about planting a seed. It's not about winning a debate. You don't need to get an answer for God on the spot. That will be between them and God—all in His perfect timing. And one last thing, witnessing is all about practice. Keep on engaging in conversations, and you'll find tremendous blessing from it.*

—Candace

A Pinch of Practicality

If you are looking for ways to share your faith, one way you can start is by giving Him the glory for your health and well-being. If someone asks you, "How did you take off the weight?" Tell them you did it God's way. This great conversation starter can lead to a discussion on faith. It can also be a great way to help another woman get healthy too.

The best way to share our faith is by being a walking and living example. So roll up your sleeves, do the best you can, and live a life that compels other people to follow the Christ you love.

Food for Thought

- I gave up all that inferior stuff so I could know Christ personally, experience his resurrection power, be a partner in his suffering, and go all the way with him to death itself. If there was any way to get in on the resurrection from the dead, I wanted to do it. I'm not saying that I have this all together, that I have it made. But I am well on my way, reaching out for Christ, who has so wondrously reached out for me. (Phil. 3:10–12 *The Message*)

- Let us, therefore, make every effort to enter that rest, so that no one will fall by following their example of disobedience. (Heb. 4:11)
- Later, knowing that all was now completed, and so that the Scripture would be fulfilled, Jesus said, "I am thirsty." A jar of wine vinegar was there, so they soaked a sponge in it, put the sponge on a stalk of the hyssop plant, and lifted it to Jesus' lips. When he had received the drink, Jesus said, "It is finished." With that, he bowed his head and gave up his spirit. (John 19:28–30)
- But I tell you that men will have to give account on the day of judgment for every careless word they have spoken. For by your words you will be acquitted, and by your words you will be condemned. (Matt. 12:36–37)
- You foolish man, do you want evidence that faith without deeds is useless? (James 2:20)
- It is God who works in you to will and to act according to his good purpose. (Phil. 2:13)
- Going a little farther, he fell with his face to the ground and prayed, "My Father, if it is possible, may this cup be taken from me. Yet not as I will, but as you will." (Matt. 26:39)
- All authority in heaven and on earth has been given to me. Therefore go and make disciples of all nations, baptizing them in the name of the Father and of the Son and of the Holy Spirit, and teaching them to obey everything I have commanded you. And surely I am with you always, to the very end of the age. (Matt. 28:18–20)
- And the times of this ignorance God winked at; but now commands all men everywhere to repent: because he has appointed a day, in the which he will judge the world in righteousness by that man whom he has ordained. (Acts 17:30–31)

The Candy Dish

I want to know how God created this world. I am not interested in this or that phenomenon, in the spectrum of this or that element. I want to know His thoughts; the rest are details. —Albert Einstein

From My Stove to Yours

Fresh Herbed Chicken Breasts

Serves 4

INGREDIENTS

4 boneless chicken breasts with skin on
2 medium cloves garlic, pressed
1 tablespoon fresh squeezed lemon juice
2 teaspoons chopped fresh sage
2 teaspoons chopped fresh thyme
1 teaspoon chopped fresh rosemary
¼ cup chicken broth
Salt and cracked black pepper

DIRECTIONS

Season the chicken breast with a little salt and pepper.

Turn oven to broil and heat to broil. Leave a metal broiling pan in there to heat.

Place the chicken in a pan and return it to broil, careful not to have the pan too high in the oven. Turn heat to low. Broil for about 15 minutes or until the chicken is done.

In the meantime prepare your herbs. Heat chopped herbs, lemon juice, broth, pressed garlic, salt, and pepper on medium for about 30 seconds.

Once chicken is done, remove the skin and slice the chicken as desired. Pour the herb mixture over chicken.

Notes

1. Phil McGraw, *The Ultimate Weight Solution: The 7 Keys to Weight Loss Freedom* (New York: Pocket Books, 2003), 44.

2. A Web site I've found helpful in teaching these principles is the Nutrition Source by Harvard School of Public Health (www.hsph.harvard.edu/nutritionsource).

3. See http://tukopamoja.wordpress.com/2009/10/25/audio-book-review-mere-christianity-by-c-s-lewis-read-by-geoffrey-howard.